D1482292

Thomas Paine

Firebrand of the Revolution

OXFORD
PORTRAITS

Thomas Paine

Firebrand of the Revolution

Harvey J. Kaye

Oxford University Press
New York • Oxford

ABV-2850

The book is dedicated to my American and British brothers-in-law, William Bauman and David Stewart

OXFORD
UNIVERSITY PRESS

Oxford New York
Athens Auckland Bangkok Bogotá Buenos Aires Calcutta
Cape Town Chennai Dar es Salaam Delhi Florence Hong Kong Istanbul
Karachi Kuala Lumpur Madrid Melbourne Mexico City Mumbai
Nairobi Paris São Paulo Singapore Taipei Tokyo Toronto Warsaw
and associated companies in
Berlin Ibadan

Copyright © 2000 by Harvey J. Kaye
Published by Oxford University Press, Inc.
198 Madison Avenue, New York, New York 10016
www.oup.com

Oxford is a registered trademark of Oxford University Press

All rights reserved. No part of this publication
may be reproduced, stored in a retrieval system, or transmitted,
in any form or by any means, electronic, mechanical,
photocopying, recording, or otherwise, without the prior
permission of Oxford University Press.

Design: Greg Wozney
Layout: Alexis Siroc
Picture research: Martin Baldessari

Library of Congress Cataloging-in-Publication Data
Kaye, Harvey J.
Thomas Paine / Harvey J. Kaye
p. cm. - (Oxford Portraits)
Summary: A biography of the political writer, with an emphasis on his contributions to the struggles of his day and their continuing relevance to modern questions.
ISBN -19-511627-5 (cloth: alk. paper)
1. Paine, Thomas, 1737–1809-Juvenile literature. 2. Political philosophers-United States-Biography-Juvenile literature. 3. Revolutionaries-United States-Biography-Juvenile literature. [1. Paine, Thomas, 1737–1809. 2. Political philosophers.] I. Title. II. Oxford portraits series.
JC178.V5 K39 1999
320.51'092-dc21
[B]
99-049395

9 8 7 6 5 4 3 2 1

Printed in the United States of America
on acid-free paper

On the cover: Portrait of Thomas Paine by Auguste Millière
Frontispiece: Engraving from the 19th-century biography *Life of Thomas Paine*

AUG 14 2000
B+T

Contents

Foreword

Ready to challenge rulers and authorities in the name of the people and democracy, Tom Paine has always been a heroic figure to me. In fact, I could not have been more than nine years old when I first discovered his writings at my grandparents' home in Brooklyn, New York.

I loved to visit my grandparents' apartment opposite the Brooklyn Museum. But there were those inevitable moments when the grownups would talk about boring subjects or about things they preferred I just didn't hear. I knew one of the latter instances was coming when one of my grandparents, both of whom had been born in Russia, would begin to speak in Yiddish, the language of eastern European Jews, so I couldn't understand. Not yet old enough to go to the museum by myself, I would escape to explore the contents of my grandparents' several rooms as if they were galleries. As my reading skills improved, I would seek out whatever books and magazines I could find, and increasingly I would end up in the dining room, where my grandfather, a trial lawyer, kept his personal library on a set of corner shelves.

Evidently, Paine fascinated my grandfather, for among a diverse assortment of works there were several by and about him. It's now quite obvious to me why. Always appreciative of a well-stated argument and critical of power holders, my grandfather was naturally drawn to the likes of Citizen Paine—and so was I. Curiously, the book that originally captured my imagination asserted that Tom Paine, not Thomas Jefferson, really authored the Declaration of Independence. However wrong the argument, I could not resist advancing it (to the obvious annoyance of my teachers).

During the next several years, I regularly returned to the radical Paine, and I came to better appreciate his unique and outstanding contributions to the making of the

American Revolution, especially through his pamphlets *Common Sense* and *The American Crisis*. Though he was never formally admitted to their ranks, I knew he deserved to be recognized as one of the Founding Fathers of the United States.

When my grandmother passed away, my grandfather moved to a smaller apartment. Recognizing my interest and eager to encourage it, he gave me a few of his Paine books to keep. Thus, as a teenager, I also read *Rights of Man,* Paine's defense of the French Revolution, and *The Age of Reason,* his critique of organized religion.

I did not "get" everything I read. To properly understand such works one has to know their historical context. Nevertheless, Paine's passion and reason impressed me. Being a working artisan before he was a writer, Paine based his democratic beliefs on experience and aspiration. He believed that the common people possessed the capacity both to comprehend the world in which they lived and to change it. Paine did not write political theory for learned elites or professors. He wrote political arguments addressed to the people, including those folks traditionally excluded from political debate and determination.

By the time I entered college in the late 1960s—a time of renewed radicalism—Paine had definitely become my hero. However, it was only in the course of my studies that I began to fully grasp the extent of his contributions to the politics and ideas of the late 18th century. Although I would still patriotically claim Paine as an American radical, I realize that he was also an Atlantic or world revolutionary. He himself insisted that he was a "citizen of the world."

My grandfather would be pleased to know that his own interest in Paine's life and legacy persists in the work of his grandson. And it seems only right that I now try to tell the story of that revolutionary writer to a younger generation.

Litho of Endicott N.Y.
The Phantom Ship
from
Legendary Ballads
BY
THOMAS MOORE
Arranged for one or three Voices
by
HENRY. R. BISHOP.
Price 50 cts
NEW YORK,
Published by FIRTH & HALL, 1, Franklin-Sq.

A privateer chases its prey on the cover of the ballad "The Phantom Ship." Opportunities for adventure, patriotism, and profit inspired many a young man to serve on board such ships in the middle of the 18th century.

CHAPTER

1

A Rebellious Age

Thomas Paine, two weeks shy of turning 20, on the verge of manhood and adult responsibilities, ran away to sea on January 17, 1757. Though he could not possibly have fathomed it at the time, this personal act of rebellion would afford him experiences and insights about the world and humanity which eventually were to express themselves in history-making ways.

Twenty years later, after many a loss and further departure, this same Tom Paine would emerge as one of the most remarkable political writers of the modern world and the greatest radical of a radical age. Through his pamphlets and other writings, such as *Common Sense*, *The American Crisis*, and *Rights of Man,* he would contribute fundamentally and mightily to the American Revolution, the French Revolution, and the struggles of English workers during the course of the Industrial Revolution.

Emanating from the laboring classes, Paine would rise to world renown and prominence, which he thoroughly enjoyed, but never to power or riches, which he never sought. Believing that men of all ranks were deserving of freedom and capable of reason, and convinced by his

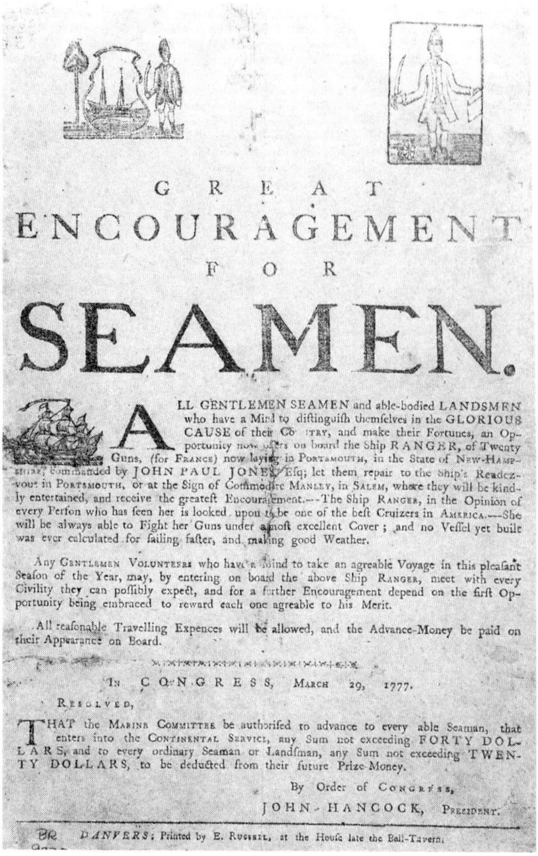
GREAT
ENCOURAGEMENT
FOR
SEAMEN.

ALL GENTLEMEN SEAMEN and able-bodied LANDSMEN who have a Mind to distinguish themselves in the GLORIOUS CAUSE of their COUNTRY, and make their Fortunes, an Opportunity now offers on board the Ship RANGER, of Twenty Guns, (for FRANCE) now laying in PORTSMOUTH, in the State of NEW-HAMPSHIRE, commanded by JOHN PAUL JONES Esq; let them repair to the Ship's Readezvous in PORTSMOUTH, or at the Sign of Commodore MANLEY, in SALEM, where they will be kindly entertained, and receive the greatest Encouragement.---The Ship RANGER, in the Opinion of every Person who has seen her is looked upon to be one of the best Cruizers in AMERICA.---She will be always able to Fight her Guns under a most excellent Cover; and no Vessel yet built was ever calculated for sailing faster, and making good Weather.

Any GENTLEMEN VOLUNTEERS who have a Mind to take an agreable Voyage in this pleasant Season of the Year, may, by entering on board the above Ship RANGER, meet with every Civility they can possibly expect, and for a further Encouragement depend on the first Opportunity being embraced to reward each one agreable to his Merit.

All reasonable Travelling Expences will be allowed, and the Advance-Money be paid on their Appearance on Board.

IN CONGRESS, MARCH 29, 1777.

RESOLVED,

THAT the MARINE COMMITTEE be authorised to advance to every able Seaman, that enters into the CONTINENTAL SERVICE, any Sum not exceeding FORTY DOLLARS, and to every ordinary Seaman or Landsman, any Sum not exceeding TWENTY DOLLARS, to be deducted from their future Prize-Money.

By Order of CONGRESS,
JOHN HANCOCK, PRESIDENT.

DANVERS: Printed by E. RUSSELL, at the House late the Bell-Tavern.

This broadside advertised openings for privateers during the American Revolution. Privateering was a means throughout the 18th century of both serving one's country and making money, since seamen were allowed to keep the spoils.

life experience that human improvement and progress were possible, he would commit himself to the realization and advancement of these ideals. Challenging the traditional authority and dogmas of kings and churches, and articulating popular aspirations for liberty, equality, and democracy, Paine's arguments would help determine the very course of modern history. His political legacy, intensely controversial in his own time, remains challenging and relevant to this day, because the ideals he advanced have yet to be fully achieved.

In the winter of 1757, however, it appears that young Tom simply wanted to escape life's routine and resist the mundane prospects it presented him. After several years of schooling, followed by more than six years working for his father as an apprentice corset maker, he felt he had to break away. In fact, he had tried to do so before, only a few months earlier, but his father had followed him down to London from their home in Norfolk and dissuaded him from sailing. On this occasion, however, Paine would not be deterred.

Tall and slim, with thick dark hair and bright eyes, and possessed of some serious learning and a pair of skilled hands, Paine signed on to the British privateer the *King of Prussia*. Commissioned by the Crown to pursue and capture enemy merchant vessels and their cargoes—or, if capture was impossible, to destroy them—privateers operated as profit-seeking enterprises. The privateers' captains and crews were entitled to keep the contents of captured vessels and divvy up the money garnered at auction. In some ways, privateering looked like piracy; but unlike piracy, privateering was considered legal and respectable, and privateers usually were less ruthless than pirates.

It is not known exactly why Paine chose the sea and privateering to assert his independence. Having spent almost all his life in his parents' home, he may have merely craved travel, action, and adventure. He may have been motivated, as well, by patriotism. The advent of the Seven Years' War (1756–63) between England and France, and the surge of nationalism it created, inspired many a youth, and privateering offered an exciting way to serve king and country. Thirty-five years later, Paine himself would recall how his "false heroism" had been "heated" by a schoolteacher's recollections of serving aboard a man-of-war. Also, making it far more attractive than regular army or naval service, privateering presented an opportunity to make good money in a relatively short time—assuming you came back alive and intact enough to enjoy it.

Adventure, patriotism, and profit were powerful recruiters. But, while enterprise encouraged the privateers, disease and death stalked them. On board, seamen endured miserable, overcrowded conditions, and almost half of those who saw combat were captured, injured or killed. Furthermore, the ships on which they sailed mirrored the oppression and exploitation of the larger world. At sea, a captain was king of his vessel, his power comparable to that of the monarchs who ruled Europe's 18th-century states. His authority at sea was personal, absolute, and, in the minds of the crewmen, all too regularly exercised in a harsh and arbitrary manner. Whatever demands Paine's schoolmasters and his father had made of him, they must have seemed nothing compared to the rigors and commands of ship life.

Foreign imprisonment, loss of limb, death—one of these fates likely would have been Paine's had his father not talked him off the privateer he originally had signed onto, the *Terrible* under the command of Captain William Death (the names alone should have been sufficient warning). In a three-hour engagement in the English Channel with the *Vengeance*, a French privateer, the *Terrible* suffered horrific losses. Out of a crew of 167, only 17 survived; every officer but one, including the captain, was killed. The *Vengeance*, too, lost its captain and two-thirds of its crew. Perhaps Paine would not have sailed on the *King of Prussia* had he known of the *Terrible*'s disastrous fate. But news of the battle only reached London after his departure. He later wrote that the *Terrible* "stood the hottest engagement of any ship" in the war.

Of course, the privateer's goal was to hunt merchant vessels and capture them with as little violence and damage as possible; and rarely could a merchant vessel stand up to a well-outfitted privateer. Thus, the privateer would usually initiate action by shooting broadsides at its prey, hoping threats alone would force a surrender; but, when the merchant ship resisted (and at least a show of resistance was standard), the privateer would position its guns to shatter the enemy's masts and sails and, with shot and splinters flying, inflict casualties. When the merchant captain eventually lowered his colors, the privateer's commander would send over a boarding party to secure the ship and sail it to a friendly port.

All hands would take a turn standing watch, and customarily, a prize was given to the man who caught first glimpse of a target. We can only guess at Paine's thoughts as he looked out across the vastness of sea and sky. Well instructed in the Bible and already intrigued by science and geography, he could not have helped wondering about the nature of the universe and marveling at the majesty of creation. At the same time, serving aboard a privateer, he must have reflected often on the extraordinary bravery and folly of men in combat and the terrible destructiveness and calamity of war.

Between hostilities, novice seamen carried out the ship's simpler tasks; however, because of his training as a corset maker, Paine presumably was assigned the more demanding job of mending sails. Looking back, he observed how more experienced seamen took it upon themselves to "instruct

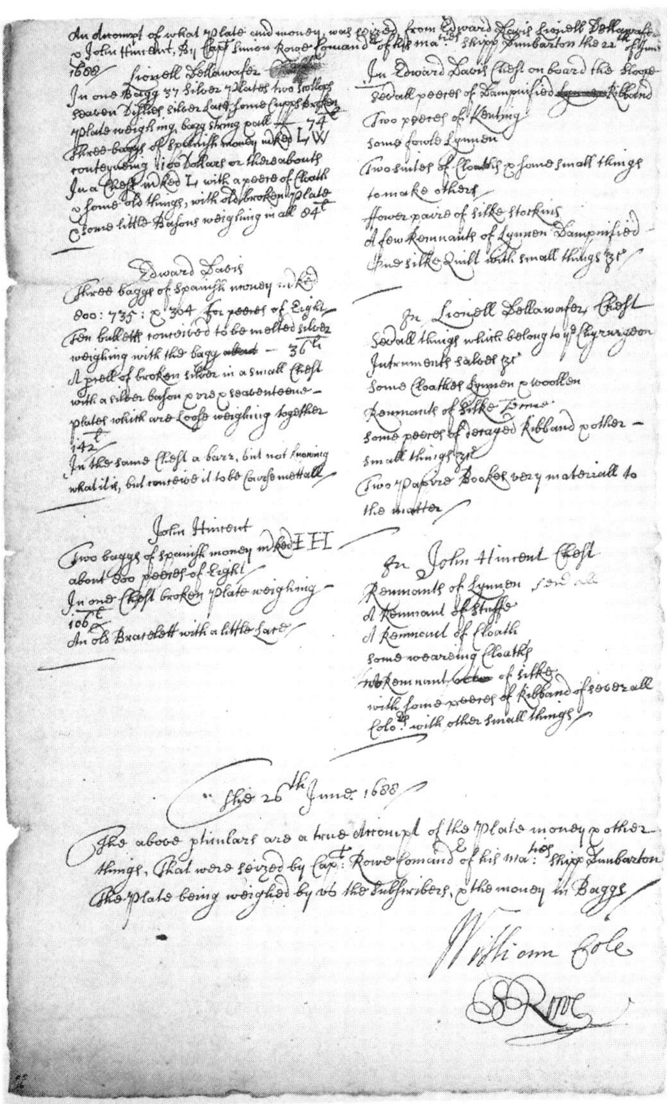
An Accompt of what Plate and money, was seized from Edward Davis Lionell Dellawafer & John Hincent, By Capt Simon Rowe Comand.r of his Ma.ties Shipp Dunbarton the 22th of June 1688

Lionell Dellawafer
In one Bagg 37 Silver Plates two Bolles seaven Dishes silver Lace some Cups Broken Plate weighing, bagg & string waight 74
Three baggs of Spanish money mark'd L W conteyning 1600 Dollars or thereabouts
In a Chest marked L with a peece of Cloath & some old things, with old broken Plate
Some little Basons weighing in all 84

Edward Davis
Three baggs of Spanish money mark'd
800 : 735 : & 364 for peeces of Eight
Ten bullett received to be melted silver weighing with the bagg about — 36
A peece of broken silver in a small Chest with a silver bason & one & seaventeene plates which are Loose weighing together 142
In the same Chest a barr, but not knowing what it is, but conceive it to be Course mettall

John Hincent
Two baggs of Spanish money mark'd I H
about 800 peeces of Eight
In one Chest broken Plate weighing 106
An old Braselett with a little Lace

In Edward Davis Chest on board the Sloope
Severall peeces of Dampnified Ribband
Two peeces of Kenting
Some fowle Lynnen
Two Suites of Cloaths & some small things to make others
Fower paire of silke stockins
A few Remnants of Lynnen Dampnified
One silke Quilt with small things &c

In Lionell Dellawafer Chest
Severall things which belong to ye Chyrurgeon Instruments salves &c
Some Cloathes Lynnen & woollen
Remnants of Silke Crape
Some peeces of Decayed Ribband & other small things &c
Two Papers Bookes very materiall to the matter

In John Hincent Chest
Remnants of Lynnen
A Remnant of Stuffe
A Remnant of Cloath
Some wearing Cloaths
A Remnant of silke with some peeces of Ribband of severall Colo.rs with other small things

The 26th June 1688
The above particulars are a true Accompt of the Plate money & other things, That were seized by Capt: Rowe Comand.r of his Ma.ties Shipp Dunbarton
The Plate being weighed by us the Subscribers, & the money in Baggs
William Cole
S Rowe

The items on this list of pirates' booty—silk, woolens, silver Spanish coins called "pieces of eight"—are similar to those one might find on a list of privateers' prizes. However, unlike pirating, which was illegal, privateering was an honorable career.

the landmen in the common work of the ship," and we know from his later comments that their comradeship and willingness to teach newcomers impressed him greatly.

Also impressive were his fellow seamen's spirited solidarity and defiant stance before the elements, the enemy, and, when their sense of justice and fairness was violated, their own captain and officers. Eighteenth-century seamen were renowned for their hostility to authority and their labor and political militancy on shore and at sea. Knowing well their crews' democratic inclinations, ships' officers had to remain persistently vigilant for potential mutinies. Paine may even have been startled at first by his comrades' directness, their vulgar language, and the clarity and forcefulness of their words. Their unity and their spirit of equality would have seemed all the more amazing to a young provincial Englishman if, as was usually the case, the *King of Prussia*'s crew was multinational or even multiracial in composition. The tides and currents of the Atlantic carried many a radical notion.

Two hundred feet in length, weighing 340 tons, and boasting two gun decks, the *King of Prussia* sailed with a sizable crew of 250. Its voyage fulfilled Paine's ambition to see action. In mid-March, several weeks out, they captured their first prize, *Le Bien Acquis.* According to the report in the official Prize Assignation Books, the ship held a cargo of "1346 Casks of Flour, 60 Barrels of Gunpowder, three 24 Pounders [cannon], three 18 Pounders, 60 Bombs, Bomb-Shells, Ammunition, Soldiers Cloaths, &c." After the prize was taken into Bristol, the cargo was sold off, and the ship was refitted as an English privateer.

Other successes quickly followed, but from mid-April to mid-June the *King of Prussia* failed to come across anything. In summer, however, a fresh series of engagements ensued. These included the rescue of two ships: the *Handy*, an Irish-owned vessel that had been in French hands for several months, and the *Pennsylvania*, which only recently, en route from London to Philadelphia, had been captured by a French privateer.

Finally, in August, the *King of Prussia* completed her cruise. Tanned and weathered, but sound and whole, Paine returned to London, endowed by his wages and share of the bounties with what must have seemed to someone of his age and background a small fortune—at least £30, about a full year's earnings for his father. Whether because of his new sense of wealth, the brutal things he had witnessed, or both, Paine did not sign on for another voyage. He had had his reasons for sailing as a privateer, and no doubt he felt he had accomplished them.

At a deeper level, going to sea surely tested and affirmed Paine's growing independence of mind, his confidence in his own worth and possibilities, and his willingness to risk everything for what he thought important—qualities he would find essential in the grander trials he still had to face. The months young Tom Paine spent "between the devil and the deep blue sea" also prepared him in ways and for developments he could not yet begin to imagine. A generation hence, his radical labors would help transform the late 18th century into the Age of Revolution.

London must have been exciting to 19-year-old Paine upon his arrival in 1756, when its streets were as boisterous with diverse people and activities as they are in this 1751 engraving by William Hogarth.

CHAPTER

2

A Freeborn English Boy

Despite her being 11 years older than Joseph Pain, Frances Cocke married him in 1734. By the time she gave birth to their first child Tom in Thetford, England, on January 29, 1737, she was 40 years old. (Tom would add the *e* to his surname on emigrating to America). Frances bore a second child, Elizabeth, a year later, but the baby girl died at the age of seven months.

Far more significant than the difference in Tom's parents' ages were the differences in their class and religious backgrounds. Class and church affiliation remain important today; but in the 1700s they carried an even greater personal and public weight, and they also determined an individual's political and social rights.

Tom's mother, the daughter of a prominent local lawyer, Thomas Cocke, was an Anglican, that is, a confirmed member of the Church of England. Tom's father, the son of a shoemaker and tenant farmer, was a skilled corset maker and a Quaker. From a very young age, his own family's circumstances would make Tom sensitive to inequality, oppression, and the possibility of reversals. Though he would not fully express it until he was middle aged, it is revealed in the poem he wrote at age eight, in memory of a pet crow:

> Here lies the body of John Crow,
> Who once was high but now is low;
> Ye brother Crows take warning all,
> For as you rise, so must you fall.

England of the mid-1700s contrasted sharply with England of the prior century and with the other states of contemporary Europe. Following the turmoil and upheaval of the 17th century, 18th-century England seemed a nation of orderliness and stability. The 1640s and 1680s, in particular, had been revolutionary decades. The 17th century witnessed civil war, the execution of the Stuart king Charles I, and the abolition of the monarchy and Anglican Church. In place of a kingdom, revolutionaries in Parliament declared the country a republic, and then a "protectorate" under their Puritan leader, Oliver Cromwell. While the forces of Parliament battled the royalists to control England, popular political and religious movements emerged. Groups such as the Levelers, Diggers, Ranters, and Quakers envisioned a more democratic England and threatened the powerful members of every party.

Only in 1660 were the monarchy and the Church of England restored under Charles II. However, conflicts persisted until 1688, when Parliament overthrew James II and replaced him with the royal couple William and Mary. Though much less tumultuous than the struggles of the 1640s, this so-called Glorious Revolution resulted in a settlement that determined the shape of the English state for the next 100 years and more, a century that saw the last of the Stuart monarchs, whose royal line originated in Scotland, and the commencement of the (originally German) House of Hanover with George I, George II, and George III.

The Glorious Revolution of 1688 transformed the Crown into a constitutional monarchy dominated by the Whig oligarchy, a ruling class of landed aristocrats and

London-based financial interests who claimed to govern in the name of Englishmen's "ancient liberties." The Whigs promoted the protection of property and Protestantism and opposed the absolute authority of the Crown and Church (for fear the latter might lead to the restoration of the Roman Catholicism they despised). Their opponents, the Tories, were no less eager to protect property, but they favored a strong royal authority and were devoted to the Church of England. In the long run, however, political principles mattered less than political spoils, the power and material benefits to be derived from possession of government offices and titles.

In 1649 revolutionaries in Parliament sentenced Charles I, King of England, to death by public beheading. With his execution, the revolutionaries intended to bring an end to monarchy in favor of a republic.

The political history of 18th-century England also includes the creation of a larger political unit, known as Great Britain. England's rulers incorporated Wales in 1536 and conquered Ireland in 1650. Finally, with the 1707 Act of Union, they brought together Scotland and England within a single state. Moreover, England's reach in the 1700s extended well beyond the British Isles to North America and the Caribbean—and there were great expectations that it would be extended even farther.

These events and ensuing developments distinguished the nation from its European counterparts. Personal, face-to-face, and dependent relations between the high- and low-born still characterized English life, as they did in other European nations. However, whereas the Continental states,

King George III contemplates a medallion of the 9th-century king Alfred the Great, a symbol that emphasized George's ancient lineage.

aside from the Dutch, were still dominated by all-powerful kings and nobles, England's revolutions had eliminated feudalism and subordinated the Crown to Parliament. English and Continental European people alike agreed: England was different. Reflecting the growth of nationalism, Englishmen boasted of their difference from and superiority to Europeans—not just because of their growing military and naval prowess but also because of their political innovations.

Members of all classes celebrated the "rights of the freeborn English" (women, too, joined the chorus, though they had less reason to do so in view of their subordinate status). Although only Anglican men were granted full civil rights—such as voting, holding public office, and attending university—the Toleration Act of 1689 accorded freedom of worship to religious Dissenters, that is, to Protestants such as Baptists and Quakers, who did not belong to the Church of England.

Nevertheless, England was a land of intensifying social inequality and oppression. Parliament was hardly constituted as a representative body. The Whig oligarchy controlled both chambers, the House of Lords and the House of Commons—the former by inheritance, the latter by patronage, including gifts, favors, and vote buying. Many a town had no representation at all, and men without property, or at least an annual income of £40, could neither vote nor hold office. Thus, out of a total population of 5 million, only 6,000 Englishmen were eligible to participate in parliamentary elections.

Compared to the past, 18th-century England was orderly and stable. Furthermore, political and economic changes were leading to evident progress and improvement, at least for the landed and monied interests who governed the country and grew ever richer as capitalism advanced. But progress regularly came at the expense of the laboring classes. In the countryside, landowning aristocrats and rural gentry proceeded to enclose their fields and modernize farming practices. To do so, they dispossessed smallholders (owners of small farms) and steadily brought an end to traditional practices such as the right to pasture animals on the village's common lands. These agrarian changes would eventually finance the Industrial Revolution. Similarly, in urban areas, merchants and shop owners responded to new opportunities by abandoning customary methods of regulating commerce and labor, such as guild restrictions on the numbers of young men allowed to enter a trade. The new political and economic order subjected people to the vagaries of the market, intensified inequalities, and created an expanding class of poor and propertyless workers.

Increasing insecurity and inequality among a people proud of their rights and freedoms, as the English were, necessarily heightens social tensions. Though a new revolution never really threatened to break out, the common people remained capable of resistance and protest, and they often made known their anger at injustices in an uproarious fashion. Indeed, excluded from official politics, 18th-century Englishmen and Englishwomen believed they had a right to express themselves through direct collective action. They drew on what they saw as time-honored rituals of rebellion and challenges to authority, actions denounced by nervous members of the upper classes as mob rule and rioting.

Intent upon preventing a return to the disorder of the previous century, England's governors managed their power and authority resolutely and effectively. When necessary, they readily resorted to force. More impressively, they established their rule by convincing the lower classes that the England in which they lived was the best of all possible societies. The Church of England played an impotant part in these efforts at social persuasion, but the law became the elites' foremost means of controlling the common folk. "Liberty" and "property" were the watchwords of Hanoverian England, and the most potent fiction of the age was that all freeborn English were equal before the law.

While the law did limit abuses by the powerful, its most important function was to instill respect for authority and the sanctity of property in those who possessed neither. Failing respect, fear would suffice.

Loathing and dreading the common people, the propertied classes imposed a savage penal code. The number of offenses punishable by death increased from 50 in 1688 to 250 a century later; they included the most minor of crimes, such as petty theft, pilfering an employer's goods, buying a stolen horse, and being out at night with a blackened face. Neither age nor sex disqualified one from hanging—women and children could be sent to the gallows, and were. As the English poet Oliver Goldsmith wrote, "Laws grind the poor, and rich men rule the law."

The England in which Tom Paine grew up was a land of social hierarchy, oppression, and antagonism. And yet, the changes underway were leading the country to capitalism, empire, and the Industrial Revolution.

Situated about 75 miles northeast of London in the county of Norfolk, Thetford was a market town during the 18th century. Dominated by the wealthy duke of Grafton and his family, the local economy remained overwhelmingly agricultural, but there was also a diverse community of artisans, to which, as a master corset maker, Tom's father belonged. Remarkably, with a population of merely 2,000—of whom only 31 could vote—the town had two seats in Parliament (both of which were controlled by the duke through vote buying and the provision of favors and jobs).

Every March, criminal court sessions convened in Thetford. For almost a week, a bizarre carnival atmosphere prevailed. Drawing great numbers to the town, there were theatricals and amusements as well as trials and executions. Most of those who suffered hanging were individuals convicted of stealing. And, overwhelmingly, they were poor, their actions probably motivated by economic desperation. Gallows Hill itself could be viewed from the Pain family cottage in the area of town known as the Wilderness. Its grisly images made a lasting impression on the young Tom, who grew up not only sympathetic to the plight of the poor but also firmly opposed to capital punishment.

An only child, Tom had a closer and more affectionate relationship with his father than his mother. And this relationship influenced him strongly. Tom early on developed a skepticism of state and religious authority, and this attitude was cultivated at home. Joseph Pain had married Frances Cocke in a Church of England ceremony and, deferring to his wife, had allowed Tom to be baptized as an Anglican. As a consequence, Joseph's Quaker brethren ostracized him. However, he never ceased to believe and think as a Quaker, and he imbued his son with Quaker values and ideas. In fact, as critical as Tom would later be of organized religion, throughout his life he regularly identified himself as a member of the Society of Friends (as the Quaker movement is called)—though, with some reason, the Friends themselves would refuse to recognize him as one of their own.

Tom Paine was born in this light-colored house in Thetford, England. The house has since been demolished to make way for the Thomas Paine Hotel.

Originating in the revolutionary 17th century under the leadership of George Fox and William Penn, the Friends rejected the formalization of religion, opposed the authority of priests, and refused to pay tithes, the official taxes paid directly to the Church. Quakers called upon people to discover the "divine spark" within themselves. Because such ideas were inherently egalitarian, and perceived as threatening by state and clerical powers, the Quakers, along with other Dissenters, were subject to official persecution from the time of the restoration in 1660 until the issuance of the Toleration Act in 1689. Though now an officially "tolerated" religious minority—a status not then accorded to Catholics and Jews—the Quakers still could not vote. Recognizing the tyranny of state churches, Tom would later declare strong support for both freedom of worship and the separation of church and state.

Other aspects of Quaker experience impressed him in a favorable way. Believing that God dwelled in every person as an inner light, Quakers saw each other as brothers and sisters. Given their sense of equality, their suspicion of authority, and their exclusion from power, they practiced mutual assistance and took care of the poorer members of their community themselves. Witnessing this, Tom came to reject hierarchies, both secular and religious, and to believe in the possibilities of collective human action.

Tom's mother raised her son in the Church of England and made sure he was taught the Bible and the Anglican catechism, the Church's central tenets or doctrines. As an adult he would keep his distance from the Church, but he pursued his boyhood study of Scripture to the point of memorizing lengthy passages. It would serve him well, both on those occasions as a young man when he would try to make a living as a preacher and later, when he would ably quote relevant biblical texts to strengthen his political and religious arguments.

Tom's parents were not affluent, but they were extremely fond of their son and committed to his receiving a formal education. As an artisan, Tom's father probably earned around £30 a year (a lower-middle-class income). Additionally, Joseph owned a small parcel of land in the country and, having been made a freeman of Thetford shortly after Tom's birth, he had pasturage rights on the town's common lands. The status of freeman also entitled Joseph and his wife to send their son to the Thetford Grammar School, just a short walk away from their cottage. Although not obliged to pay registration fees, Tom's parents did have to cover the cost of supplies. In addition, Tom's school attendance meant he would not be adding to the family income by working. Fortunately for Tom, in addition to his parents' willingness to make sacrifices, his mother's sister was prepared to help out.

Thetford Grammar School had been founded in 1566. During Tom's student days, the school separated the boys into two curricular groups. Those pupils aspiring to professional careers learned Latin along with their other studies; those destined for livelihoods in the trades did not. Tom's parents enrolled him in the latter group, not because he was incapable of mastering Latin or because they had limited expectations of him; rather, his father drew the line at a Latin education. Quakers believed that Latin, the official language of states and churches, served to obscure the exercise of power and authority from the people. Tom would look back 40 years later and recall, rather immodestly:

> I did not learn Latin, not only because I had no inclination to learn languages, but because of the objection the Quakers have against the books in which the language is taught. But this did not prevent me from being acquainted with the subjects of all the Latin books used in the school.

(Arguably, Tom's ignorance of Latin turned out to be a good thing because, as a radical pamphleteer hoping to engage the popular imagination, it kept him from fancifying his words and putting off working people.)

Tom excelled at mathematics, and his favorite subjects were science and poetry. They became lifelong pursuits, and in spite of his accomplishments as a political writer, Paine himself always claimed the "natural bent of my mind was to science." On the literary and poetic side, he enjoyed reading the works of John Milton, John Bunyan, and William Shakespeare. Inspired by these authors, Tom often spent time writing his own verses, something his parents tried to discourage in favor of seemingly more practical activities. (Reading Milton and Bunyan also apparently nourished his later political and religious radicalism.)

One of Tom's teachers, the Reverend William Knowles, had served as a chaplain aboard an English warship. Firing the boy's youthful imagination, Knowles regaled him with stories of sailing out to India and then back around Africa to the West Indies and North America. Also, Tom read several popular adventurers' tales and books about America, including a history of Virginia. These gave him ideas of traveling abroad and of perhaps one day crossing the Atlantic. But his family had other plans for him.

Eighteenth-century aristocratic women wore bone stays to make their waists appear tiny. Though this illustration humorously portrays a dressing scene, the practice threatened the health of fashion-conscious women.

In 1750, when he turned 13, Tom's parents withdrew him from school and apprenticed him to his father to learn the craft of corset making or, as it was also known, stay making, for it entailed the making of stays for the woolen-cloth corsets of upper-class women. Usually made of whalebone, stays were stiffeners used to reshape a woman's figure and (rigorously) provide the wearer with an hourglass-shaped figure. Laborious work, making stays demanded skilled hands, concentration, and patience.

Tom worked with his father as an apprentice for six years. Considering the many hours they spent together in the shop, Tom's father no doubt spoke to him at length of the Quakers' dissenting and egalitarian spirit and passed on to him historical memories of "turning the world upside down" in the revolutionary 1640s and 1650s.

Thetford's smallish size afforded only a limited market for stay makers' wares. Therefore, for a brief period Tom went to work for a cousin in a town several miles away. Yet, with growing competition from London, the local economic picture did not improve, and there was serious doubt about Tom's being able to join his father as a partner in the shop.

Whether because of the bleak business opportunities, or Tom's own eagerness to see something of the larger world, he left his parents' household in 1756 to work in London as a journeyman stay maker, the next step following an apprenticeship in the process of becoming a master craftsman. Through his father's contacts in the trade, Tom secured employment in the capital with John Morris, a master artisan, who resided at the heart of the city, in Covent Garden, a boisterous commercial district that was the site of London's largest fruit and vegetable market—and increasingly the center of the city's nightlife.

Whatever anxieties he had about the move—and even if his projected labors promised more of the arduous routine he knew at home—Tom must have been ecstatic on arrival in the capital. London's streets and shops were filled with diverse peoples and goods, not just from every corner of the British Isles but also from the Continent, the lands of the Mediterranean and the Orient, and the varied shores of the Atlantic. Encountering so many new and wondrous things, any young Englishman would have found the city exotic and thrilling.

However, as exciting as London might have been, its dangers and delights only served to stoke Tom's desires for travel and adventure. Twice that same year, he resolved that he would run away to serve aboard a privateer. The second time, he sailed.

The capital of an expanding empire, London, with a population of 600,000, grew out from the River Thames, which snakes across the lower half of this 1760 map.

CHAPTER

3

A Young Man's Travails

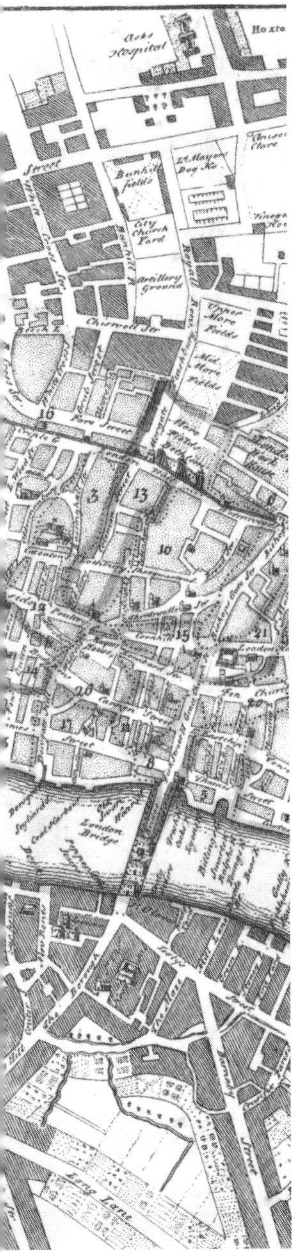

After eight months at sea, Tom Paine returned to London, tanned and fit, his hair long and tied back in a ponytail. Having survived both combat and the elements, he no doubt felt himself fortunate. Richer in pocket and experience than when he left, he surely believed the future held great things for him. However, while many challenges and occasional moments of joy and achievement would present themselves, the next 17 years of Paine's life would more often entail tragedy and failure. He would never fully overcome his pain over the most personal and intimate of all his losses. Yet, in the course of these years, he would learn much about the political and social world, and he would develop skills and ideas critically equipping him for the public struggles to which he would ultimately commit himself.

Back in London, Paine's earnings as a privateer freed him from worrying about employment, at least for a while. Thus, he set out to improve himself and to explore the scientific questions that so intrigued him. Taking lodgings in Covent Garden, he spent a good bit of time in bookshops. He also bought a set of globes and charts and started attending lectures on subjects such as astronomy and geography.

With a population greater than 600,000, London was the capital of an expanding empire. However, in contrast to other European capitals, it lacked an institution of higher learning. Perhaps that was just as well. England's universities, Oxford and Cambridge, were archaic, offering degrees only in theology and the classics. The absence of medieval colleges allowed London's intellectual life to be all the more modern and democratic in character, and its growing middle and artisan classes—excluded from university for reasons of social status, gender, or religion—supported a thriving number of publishers, bookshops, periodicals, and lectures.

Independent lecturers, such as Paine's favorites, the spectacle maker Benjamin Martin and the astronomer James Ferguson, were usually self-taught, skilled artisans. And, like Paine himself, those attending the presentations and demonstrations of these men, and joining in the tavern and coffeehouse discussions that followed, were usually lower-middle-class Dissenters eager for self-improvement.

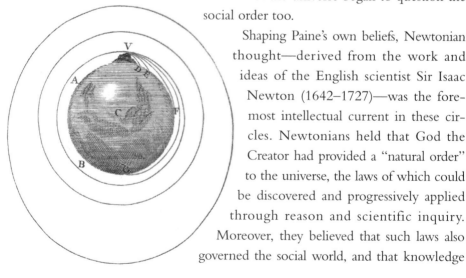

Through reason and a scientific approach, Isaac Newton demonstrated in this diagram how the moon orbits the earth. Paine believed that the "natural order" discovered by Newton governed not only the universe but society as well.

Paine not only found himself among people of similar background who avidly shared his interests. He also found himself within a new culture of political radicalism. Those who stood outside the official church and questioned nature and the order of the universe began to question the social order too.

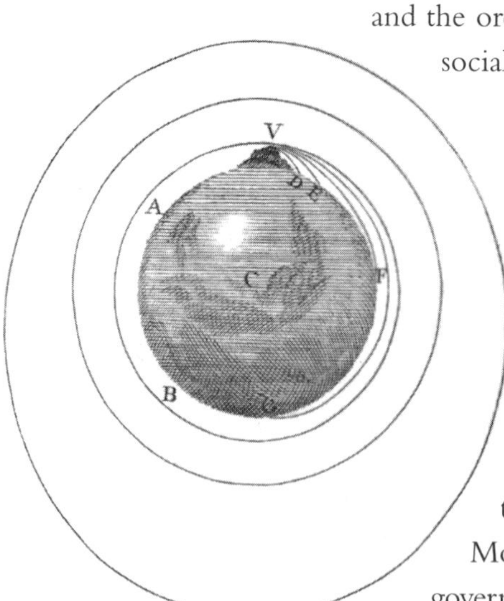

Shaping Paine's own beliefs, Newtonian thought—derived from the work and ideas of the English scientist Sir Isaac Newton (1642–1727)—was the foremost intellectual current in these circles. Newtonians held that God the Creator had provided a "natural order" to the universe, the laws of which could be discovered and progressively applied through reason and scientific inquiry. Moreover, they believed that such laws also governed the social world, and that knowledge of them could guide the reform and improvement of human institutions. Aware of the implications, government and Church authorities grew anxious and kept a watchful eye on those espousing such ideas.

John Wesley founded the Methodist movement, which attracted Paine in the late 1750s. Wesley intended Methodism to spiritually reinvigorate the Church of England, but in 1791 it became a separate church.

Paine could remain a "student" only so long. By the spring of 1758 he needed to find work. Moving out of London to Sandwich, 75 miles to the southeast, he set himself up as a master stay maker. In Sandwich, Paine became involved in the Methodist movement and even took to preaching. Whatever reservations he had about organized religions' ties to power, and the limitations they set to thought and imagination, Methodist ideas and practices impressed him. Intended as a campaign to reinvigorate the people's Christian spirit, Methodism originated within the Church of England under John Wesley's leadership. Proposing that every individual could be saved (in contrast to the Puritan and Calvinist belief that only the preordained "elect" were destined for heaven), Methodism offered hope in times of difficulty and change. The movement grew rapidly, especially among the lower classes.

Though begun as a mission to bring the common people back into the Church of England, Methodism was developing into an alternative to the Anglican faith. Paine recognized in Methodism many of the things he admired about the Society of Friends, including an essential egalitarianism and solidarity. Like the Quakers, Methodists taught that salvation depended on individual choice and action. To be a good Christian, a person had not only to discover God but also do good works and be concerned about the welfare of others. Methodism called for self-discipline but—as a revival movement bringing people together in religious gatherings—also afforded community and mutual support. Furthermore, even though Methodists propagated a conservative message, the founding of a Methodist chapel was a rebellious act. Indeed, chapel life furnished important political and educational experiences. Creating and maintaining a chapel meant learning skills of organization and self-governance. And by promoting Bible study, Methodism cultivated reading, writing, and public speaking among the otherwise illiterate.

What Paine witnessed among the Methodists encouraged his emergent belief in the potential of the common people. And preaching to Methodist gatherings compelled him to cultivate his own verbal skills in a popular and persuasive manner.

In the spring of 1759, Paine met Mary Lambert, with whom he fell in love. Known as a "pretty girl of modest behavior," Lambert worked as a maid in the home of a prominent local family. Not much more is known about her, other than the sad fact that she had been orphaned as a child.

Paine and Lambert married in St. Peter's Church on September 27. However happy they were, life would have it otherwise. Mary soon became pregnant and, unfortunately, Tom's corset-making shop failed for lack of business. In early 1760, in hopes of starting over—and believing the sea air would be better for Mary's health—they moved to Margate, on the southeast coast. That summer, Mary went into a difficult labor, and both she and the baby died. Such losses were not uncommon, for medical and birthing practices were relatively primitive, especially for the poor. But these deaths were always tragic.

At 23, Paine was alone and almost penniless. There is no record of his exact feelings. Like most other men of the time, he did not write or speak much of his grief but, rather, bore it silently. He would marry again, but he would never really love another woman.

Paine could not, and did not, sit still. Mary's late father had been an excise officer—an assessor and collector of the excise, a national tax applied to an array of consumer goods—and she and Paine had discussed the idea of Paine seeking such employment. Hoping for his parents' support, he now wrote his father, setting out his intentions. Receiving a favorable reply, he returned to Thetford in the spring of 1761 and prepared for the required entrance examinations.

Paine was fortunate. Not only were his parents willing to help, but so was his grandfather. A lawyer, Thomas Cocke used his contacts in government and the duke of Grafton's household to secure assistance for his grandson. In a society of hierarchy and patronage, connections were essential. Tutored for the tests, steered through the bureaucratic hurdles and possibly aided by the duke's own intervention, Paine gained appointment as an "unattached officer," supplying him a small salary while he awaited his first posting.

In December 1762, the Excise Commission directed Paine to Grantham in Lincolnshire, a town of the North Midlands situated about 120 miles north of London, to serve as an apprentice officer. Limited to gauging brewers' casks, the assignment quickly bored him, but he persevered, and in the summer of 1764 the commission offered him a promotion and transfer to the Alford Outride on the North Sea coast. Alford had a reputation as a tough and dangerous post. In addition to tax assessing and collecting, the station officer had to patrol the shore on horseback, watching out for smugglers. A booming enterprise, smuggling constituted up to half of 18th-century British trade.

Taxmen are hardly ever welcome. The addition of policing functions to their duties made it a highly unpopular career, especially around Alford, where many locals relied upon smuggling for extra income. Nevertheless, eager for the challenge and a salary increase, Paine grabbed the offer.

Because the work involved a variety of activities, Paine enjoyed it. Yet his best efforts were undone when he was accused of laziness and incompetence. Specifically, he was charged with "stamping" goods he had not inspected, that is, with assigning tax values without actually checking the quantities and contents of casks and containers. In August 1765, he was dismissed.

Given the low wages, heavy demands, and unpopularity of excisemen, stamping was a fairly widespread practice. But was Paine actually guilty? It long has been assumed so; yet a closer look at the events surrounding the case reveals he might not have been. For a start, Paine might have wrongly believed that an admission of guilt afforded the best chance to avoid getting fired. More crucially, it appears Paine might actually have been framed by his supervisor, William Swallow, in an attempt by Swallow to cover up his own corruption. In fact, the Excise Commission discharged Swallow only several weeks after Paine. It is even possible that Paine knew of Swallow's dirty dealing but, given the system of authority, felt incapable of doing anything about it. In any case, Paine was personally aggrieved by the state's injustice, and he resolved to get himself reinstated.

Shamed and unemployed, Paine returned to Thetford and once more sought the aid of his family. But after a frustrating winter, he decided to go to London and directly petition the Excise Commission. Deferentially, he composed a letter pleading for reinstatement.

In July 1766, Paine's petition succeeded. However, it would take another 18 months to secure a suitable posting. In the meantime, he had to make a living. Staying in London, but abandoning stay making, he eked out an income by teaching at schools for children of the working classes. Though he barely made enough to survive, his experience further persuaded him of the value of education for all children, boys and girls alike. In addition, he again took to preaching at Methodist gatherings, and he renewed his ties among the city's scientific and intellectual community which, fortuitously, led to his meeting the renowned American writer, scientist, and inventor Benjamin Franklin.

An economic depression in the 1760s made life all the more difficult for working people. Harvests failed, prices rose, wages lagged, and, in the wake of the Seven Years'

A portrait of John Wilkes adorned the cover of the Boston Almanack *for 1769. Roused by the government's prosecution of Wilkes for printing "seditious libel" against the king and his ministers, the common people celebrated him with cries of "Wilkes and Liberty!"*

War, unemployment increased; plus Atlantic trade fell off as a consequence of increasing American antagonism to British colonial policies. Popular anger sought outlets, and disturbances broke out across the country.

London experienced a wave of industrial disputes and crowd actions, including rallies in support of John Wilkes, a Member of Parliament in the House of Commons. The publisher of the newspaper the *North Briton*, Wilkes was being prosecuted—or, as many thought, persecuted—by the government for printing "seditious libel against George III and his ministers." A wit and a scoundrel, Wilkes himself was more than prepared to exploit crowd sympathies to advance his own cause. Nevertheless, the middle- and working-class folk in the streets shouting "Wilkes and Liberty!" saw great matters at stake in his case, perceiving an ominous example of government menacing the rights of freeborn Englishmen. Paine could not have failed to notice such protests and the budding radicalism of those who participated.

Finally, in February 1768, Paine received a posting to Lewes in Sussex. With a population of 4,000, a vigorous public life, several Nonconformist churches, and a tradition of opposition to the monarchy and pro-republican sentiments going back to the revolutionary decades of the 17th century, Lewes must have seemed inviting. Paine immediately found lodging with tobacconist Samuel Ollive, his wife, Esther, and their daughter, Elizabeth, a bright and pretty 20-year old who ran a local boarding school for girls. (The Ollives also had three grown sons.) A town constable, Samuel took an immediate liking to Paine and enthusiastically introduced him around town.

Paine was a friendly and sociable young man, and with Ollive's endorsement he soon became directly engaged in town life. Though an excise officer, he came to be so well liked he was elected to the Society of Twelve, the town

text continues on page 38

GENERAL OF THE HEADSTRONG WAR

Paine's associates in the Headstrong Club fully appreciated his company and his arguments during their regular social gatherings at the White Hart Inn in Lewes. Years later, fellow club member William Lee wrote in the Sussex Weekly Advertiser, or Lewes Journal *(January 13, 1794) that Paine had been a "shrewd and sensible fellow" who possessed an impressive "depth of political knowledge." Lee himself had composed a mock—but truly appreciative—eulogy for Paine in which he dubbed him the "General of the Headstrong War."*

Immortal PAINE! while mighty reasoners jar,
We crown thee General of the Headstrong War;
Thy logic vanquish'd error, and thy mind
No bounds, but those of right and truth, confined.
Thy soul of fire must sure ascend the sky,
Immortal PAINE, thy fame can never die;
For men like thee their names must ever save
From the black edicts of the tyrant grave.

council. It gave him his first experience as a self-governing citizen rather than merely a royal subject. He also served on the vestry, the church committee supervising the disbursement of parish taxes and aid to the poor.

Paine's engagements extended in a more social direction as well. His ice-skating skills garnered him the nickname the Commodore. More pivotally, he became a regular member of the Headstrong Club, a drinking, eating, and discussion group that met at the White Hart Inn. In this company he began to articulate his increasingly critical political views.

Following rounds of the local ale and a plate of oysters, Paine energetically argued the issues of the day (including, presumably, the state of the American colonies) and gained a name as a superb debater. His comrades appreciated him and occasionally honored his performances by granting him the prized custody of the Headstrong Book, the club's minutes. A young friend and, later, biographer, Thomas "Clio" Rickman, recalled that Paine spoke as a Whig and was "notorious for that quality which has been defined perseverance in a good cause and obstinacy in a bad one. He was tenacious of his opinions, which were bold, acute, and independent, and which he maintained with ardour, elegance, and argument."

Sussex periodicals often printed articles critical of government and the power structure. Writing under a pseudonym, as was the custom, Paine is believed to have penned columns and letters discussing "liberty of the press" and "religious bigotry." Most definitely, he composed pieces for the Headstrong Club, one of which smartly challenged the prevailing belief that existing social inequalities were inevitable.

Paine's friend and mentor, Samuel Ollive, died in July 1769. For the sake of propriety, Paine moved out of the Ollive home. But he remained close to the family and, at the invitation of Esther Ollive, took over responsibility for the tobacco shop. With Esther's encouragement, he also grew closer to her daughter, Elizabeth. He felt a special attachment to the family, and in time, he proposed to Elizabeth. They married on March 26, 1771. The couple seemed happy together, but ensuing events caused severe problems in their relationship.

Excise officers were a poorly paid lot pursuing a dangerous livelihood with a great deal of work and responsibility. In 1772, increasingly resentful of their impoverished circumstances, Paine and his colleagues in the Sussex area banded together to formally request a salary increase from Parliament. Paine's growing reputation for a skill with words led his fellow officers to commission him to write their petition. That summer Paine authored his first pamphlet, bluntly titled *The Case of the Officers of Excise.* Clearly written, the petition presents the case for a raise in terms of the needs of the men and their families, the arduousness of the work, the risk of poverty breeding corruption within the staff, and the imperative of recruiting well-qualified officers. Almost every one of the excise service's 3,000 officers signed on and paid a small subscription to send Paine to London to press their demands among Members of Parliament. So authorized, Paine headed to the capital and spent the winter of 1772–73 advancing the excisemen's cause. He must have believed that his efforts would meet with at least some success. Early in the text he calmly observes, "There are some cases so singularly reasonable, that the more they are considered the more weight they obtain."

Unfortunately, Paine's mission suffered utter defeat. Making it all the worse, his labors cost him everything he had. The tobacco shop failed for lack of proper attention. The Excise Commission sacked him for abandoning his post. And his marriage collapsed.

It is said that Paine did not truly love Elizabeth; rumors even claimed that the two of them had never consummated their vows. In any case, the couple agreed to separate. Neither one of them was to remarry. Following the separation, Elizabeth went to live with a brother and his family and made a small living as a dressmaker. Looking back, Paine always spoke fondly of her, but he persistently refused to discuss the breakup, stating simply that there was "a cause, which is nobody's business." Though he had no further direct contact with Elizabeth, in years to come he occasionally sent small sums of money to her brother for her maintenance. She died in July 1808.

Thirty-seven years old, with a history of defeats and nothing left for him in Lewes, Paine returned to London, figuring that he could at least spend time in the places and among the people he so relished. The only apparent good that had come of the months he had passed in the capital on behalf of his fellow excise officers was the opportunity to renew scientific and intellectual acquaintances. There he reencountered Benjamin Franklin, now in London representing the cause of the increasingly agitated and rebellious American colonies. Sympathetic to Paine's worsened circumstances, Franklin spoke encouragingly to him about going to America.

In September 1774, with a letter of introduction from Franklin, Paine boarded ship for America. The letter—directed to Franklin's son-in-law, Richard Bache, a well-to-do insurance underwriter in Philadelphia, and his son, William Franklin, then Royal governor of New Jersey—read:

> The bearer, Mr. Thomas Pain, is very well recommended to me as an ingenious worthy young man. He goes to Pennsylvania with a view of settling there. I request you to give him your best advice and countenance, as he is quite a stranger there. If you can put him in a way of obtaining employment as a clerk, or assistant tutor in a school, or assistant surveyor (of all of which I think him very capable) so that he may procure a subsistence at

> least, til he can make acquaintance and obtain a knowledge of the country you will do well and much oblige your affectionate father.

Franklin's words are supportive, but they do not reveal great expectations. Why should they? Penniless and without real prospects, though possessed of a seemingly indefatigable spirit, Paine merely aspired to situate himself and, perhaps, establish a school for girls. Little did either man suspect that the mix of historical and personal memories and skills that Paine carried with him would be so volatile when brought into contact with American developments and possibilities.

With a population of 30,000, Philadelphia served as the economic and cultural capital of British North America, and with the convening of the Continental Congress in 1774, it became its political capital as well.

CHAPTER

4

AMERICA

Tom Paine's adult life thus far had been a series of failures and scandals. Nevertheless, he looked forward to starting over in America, and more than he ever could have imagined, America would grant him a new beginning. What he was to discover in the "new world" would remind him that, as tragic as history all too often is, it also presents surprising opportunities and challenges for great change and progress. America would inspire Paine, and seeking to engage the possibilities he perceived, he would refashion his own life and contribute, as well, to the refashioning of America. Little more than a year after landing, he was to declare, "We have it in our power to begin the world over again." These words were destined to fire the imaginations of his new compatriots.

The America to which Paine journeyed was thriving, dynamic, and rebellious. After growing rapidly, the population of the 13 colonies had reached almost 3 million by the 1770s. The vast majority of people lived in the countryside, but Boston, New York, Philadelphia, and Charleston had developed relatively sophisticated economies, social activities, and cultural entertainment. These cities had become prosperous regional capitals, linking their respective regions to Britain and the larger world, both sides of the Atlantic Ocean, especially western Europe and the Caribbean islands.

Colonial life did not simply reflect life in the mother country. Though Americans were even more pro-monarchy in their sympathies than the English, with the king and his ministers an ocean away they could afford to be. While rich gentlemen might lord it over others, actual aristocrats were a rare breed in America. And though religious toleration varied from colony to colony, the Church of England never secured the authority it held at home. Rather, religious pluralism and religious enthusiasm characterized American life. Moreover, in contrast to Britain, America had little unemployment or poverty. The agrarian dream meant owning the land you worked, and the majority did. Although the same basic qualification to vote—ownership of property—applied in America as in Britain, the colonies were far more democratic places. More than half of colonial white men possessed sufficient property to vote; they governed themselves through elected assemblies (subject to the veto power of royal governors); and they enjoyed the freest press of the 18th century. Like their British cousins, colonials celebrated their liberties—arguably, they had even more reason to do so—and, while excluded from high political debate, the middling and lower classes registered their views through crowd actions.

America seemed exceptional, yet serious contradictions marked the developing society. Fundamental inequalities shaped colonial life, and antagonisms were intensifying. Women's lives varied according to their social class and marital status, but all suffered the restrictions of male domination. Colonials prided themselves on their liberties, but their economies depended upon denying freedom to others. To gain passage to America, poor white immigrants subjected themselves to indentured servitude, bound to labor for their masters for several years in repayment of the cost of their voyages. More cruelly, a vicious transatlantic trade brought Africans to work and die as slaves, and by the mid-1770s they numbered half a million. The rebelliousness of servants and slaves distressed their masters. Alongside the colonials, and in far greater numbers in the interior, lived the Native American peoples, determined to withstand European expansion as best they could.

Real inequalities also prevailed among free white colonials. Sorely reminding everyone of the British landscape, large landholdings grew, giving rise to a system of landlordism and tenantry; the abuses of this system periodically incited tenant farmers to riot in protest. Property also shaped urban life. Wealthy merchants, upon whose transactions practically every other class depended, had built their fortunes on transatlantic commerce. Together with the rural elites—the Southern planters and Northern landlords—they constituted provincial ruling classes and dominated colonial assemblies. On the next social level, beneath these ruling classes but closely connected to them, was an intellectual elite made up of lawyers and prominent Protestant clergy.

Of course, the majority of those who lived in towns and cities belonged to the working classes. Skilled artisans of diverse trades, known as master mechanics, owned their own shops and hired journeymen and apprentices, the men and boys who comprised the middle and entry levels of the artisan ranks. These were Tom Paine's folk. Literate and often interested in science and public affairs, artisans aspired to an independent livelihood and community respect gained through hard work, moderation, and self-improvement. Combining the roles of employer and worker, consumer and manufacturer, master artisans increasingly felt the strains of colonial life and sought a greater role in determining colonial developments.

Below the artisans on the social scale, propertyless laborers grew in number, including sailors, dock workers, hired servants, and the unskilled. Though better off in America than in Britain, they knew well that they lacked the rights of the propertied classes, and they could see the rich growing richer. Their rising sense of injustice, and their readiness to express it, made colonial elites nervous.

What held the colonials together and bound them to the empire was their shared "Britishness" (though significantly, not all colonials were actually British or even of British descent). In spite of the glaring contradictions in colonial society, they had reason to believe—as did their British counterparts—that they enjoyed rights other peoples did not have, rights secured through the ages and assured by the British constitution. Ironically, the very demands of maintaining an empire would soon strain the colonials' ties to the British Empire, the monarchy, and finally their sense of Britishness.

Britain's triumph in the Seven Years' War—known in America as the French and Indian War (1756–63) because British and Americans together fought the French and their Indian allies—drove the French from Canada and secured British domination of North America and the Atlantic world. But victory and supremacy bore a high price, exhausting the treasury and forcing the British government to raise taxes and seek additional sources of income. King George III and his chief financial minister, George Grenville, logically assumed that the costs of colonial security should be borne by the colonials themselves—an assumption the latter did not share, feeling they had paid for the North American war with their blood. The Government also sought to more effectively regulate American commerce to Britain's advantage, and to intervene between white colonists and Native Americans to protect the latter's treaty rights from the colonists' greed for new lands to invest in and settle. The resulting policies instigated a series of imperial crises.

Frustrating many a colonial's ambitions, in 1763 Grenville laid out a "Proclamation Line" along the

Appalachian Mountains, restricting white territorial expansion to the west. And during the next decade he and his successors announced a string of new taxes and regulations governing colonial commerce and administration: the Sugar Act (1764), the Stamp Act (1765), the Quartering Act (1765), the Declaratory Act (1766), the Townshend Acts (1767), the Tea Act (1773), and the so-called Coercive or Intolerable Acts (1774).

The British government believed that the British constitution (a collection of laws enacted over the centuries, rather than a single document) gave it the authority to make laws for the colonies in all cases, because all freeborn Englishmen were understood to be "represented" in Parliament whether or not they actually voted for members of the House of Commons. By contrast, most American colonists believed that Parliament was acting in an arbitrary and unconstitutional way, and that Parliament and the government were violating the colonials' rights as Englishmen by making laws without their consent. Beginning in 1765, the argument between Britain and its American colonies unfolded, in good part, as a dispute between these two positions. By 1775, the dispute reached a stalemate that Paine would play a vital role in shattering.

Angered by the stance of the British government, colonial leaders delivered speeches and wrote pamphlets decrying tyranny and the threat to liberty. They worried about agitating the masses but, by tapping into popular sentiments, their own words and actions did just that. And once mobilized, middle- and lower-class folk grew less and less willing to defer to their "betters." They gathered in street protests, hung figures in effigy, and attacked British officials and their property. In time, they would propel the elites into action.

American defiance made the colonial system unworkable, repeatedly leading Parliament to repeal its latest revenue-raising law. However, Parliament continued to levy

new taxes. In turn, the colonials staged boycotts of British-made goods and events such as the Boston Tea Party (1773), in which a group of colonials, disguised as Indians, dumped a shipment of British tea into Boston Harbor. Occasionally, there were violent confrontations, such as the Boston Massacre of 1770; on the damp, chilly night of March 5, British troops killed four men when they fired on a crowd that had gathered to taunt them. Resistance escalated with every new confrontation. Colonials organized, first locally and then across colonial lines. In the 1760s, Bostonian Samuel Adams had recruited artisans, smaller merchants, and dissident intellectuals such as his cousin, the lawyer John Adams, into the Sons of Liberty; in the early 1770s, Committees of Correspondence formed in all the colonies to assure a continuous flow of information in support of resistance efforts.

In 1764, the British government began to impose a series of taxes and regulations on the American colonists. Americans took to the streets to protest the 1765 Stamp Act.

By 1774 the dispute between Britain and America had become a full-blown constitutional crisis. It came to a head when Parliament passed the so-called Coercive or Intolerable Acts, which closed Boston Harbor and essentially placed Boston and the Massachusetts colony under siege. Outraged, the colonies sent delegates to Philadelphia for the First Continental Congress in September 1774. They promised aid to Massachusetts, called for a continental boycott of British goods, and issued a declaration against "taxation without representation." Meanwhile, colonial militias trained more seriously, and the Massachusetts Minutemen readied themselves for action. The British had united the colonials in rebellion.

It was at this time that Paine sailed to America aboard the *London Packet*, landing in Philadelphia only weeks after the First Continental Congress adjourned. The eight-week voyage hardly augured well for his future. Following the usual seasickness, a deadly epidemic known as "ship fever," probably typhus, overtook passengers and crew alike. When the *London Packet* docked on November 30, 1774, Paine had to be carried ashore on a stretcher and spent the next several weeks recuperating.

Given his past history, Paine was remarkably fortunate, and not just for having survived the journey. Travelling as a free man, with money and Benjamin Franklin's letter of introduction in his purse, his status contrasted sharply with that of the majority of new arrivals. One hundred of the 120 passengers with whom he had sailed were indentured servants, and the Philadelphia Slave Market could easily be seen from his rented lodgings in the heart of the city.

In early January Paine roused himself to get out and about. Doing so helped further reinvigorate him. Though only a square mile in size, Philadelphia, with a fast-growing population of 30,000 and America's busiest harbor, had emerged as the unofficial commercial and cultural capital of British North America. The city's prosperity and ethnic and religious diversity clearly impressed Paine. Founded by the Quaker William Penn, the Pennsylvania colony had been a haven for the Friends, and Philadelphia reflected its Quaker heritage. Its European population included native and immigrant English Quakers, Anglicans and Catholics, German Lutherans and Mennonites, Scotch-Irish Presbyterians, and Jews.

Philadelphia's politics also appealed to Paine. Aristocratic in wealth and demeanor, the merchant elite controlled economic affairs and colonial government. However, they faced challenges from below. Independent minded and egalitarian in spirit, the mechanics—the skilled workers who made up half the city's population—had long resented the merchants' domination. Now, further antagonized by British taxes and restrictions, they insisted upon a direct role in government. Not only the wealthier artisans, but also the poorer artisans and laborers, many of whom had enlisted in Pennsylvania's militia, began to demand the right of political participation. Such things thrilled Paine, and yet the paradox of white servitude and black bondage in the midst of a prosperous, liberty-loving, and spirited people astounded him.

Franklin's letter enabled Paine to meet influential people. A Philadelphia artisan who had become an international celebrity, Franklin was beloved by the city's working people and, as the author of *Poor Richard's Almanack,* widely recognized as the "voice of the people." As Franklin had directed, Paine first arranged to meet Richard Bache, who, taking a liking to the new arrival, promised both to help him find employment as a tutor and to introduce him to the city's leading figures.

By the early 1730s Poor Richard's Almanack *had become the second-most popular book in the colonies, after the Bible. It contained entertaining but wise advice and popular philosophy, as in this illustrated maxim.*

As in London, Paine quickly took to spending time in bookshops. One afternoon, the owner of his favorite shop, Robert Aitken, engaged him in conversation about his literary interests, leading Paine to show him several of his own writings. After he perused them, Aitken amazed Paine by offering him the editorship of the *Pennsylvania Magazine,* a new periodical he planned to copublish with John Witherspoon, the president of the College of New Jersey (later renamed Princeton University). Incredibly, only weeks off the ship, Paine had a new career as a journalist.

The first issue appeared on January 24, 1775. The magazine flourished. Paine himself contributed essays, poems, and scientific reports, written, as was the custom, under various pseudonyms, such as "Atlanticus," "Vox Populi" (The People's Voice), and "Justice and Humanity." Expressing his renewed optimism and progressive view of the future, Paine developed a public voice—a writing style and vocabulary—in tune with the promise he sensed in American life. In his opening editorial he warned against "historical superiority," the idea that the present age represents the highest and final stage of history.

Appreciating American possibilities, Paine also confronted America's contradictions. He criticized aristocratic and lordly pomposity. In one essay he considered the oppression of women. In yet another, "African Slavery in America," published in the *Pennsylvania Journal and the Weekly Advertiser,* he vigorously attacked slavery, calling for its abolition and insisting upon America's responsibility to support the slaves following emancipation. Not long after, Franklin returned to Philadelphia and established the first American Anti-Slavery Society, with Paine as a founding member.

Paine wrote critically of the way Britain exercised imperial power and control over America and Americans, but he favored reconciliation—until April 19, 1775, when British troops opened fire on American militiamen at Lexington, Massachusetts, leaving 8 dead and 10 wounded. News of the Battle of Lexington—"the shot heard round the world"—turned Paine into an American patriot and radical writer. Forsaking his Quaker background, he argued in "Thoughts on Defensive War" that violence was legitimate in defense of liberty; and in the poetic verses of a

text continues on page 54

"The Liberty Tree," 1775

During his first several months in America, Paine wrote critically of British imperialism and colonialism, but it was not until after the Battles of Lexington and Concord in April 1775 that Paine publicly committed himself to the American rebellion. Interested in poetry and poetic composition ever since his boyhood schooldays, Paine penned his new allegiance to America in the song "The Liberty Tree."

A Song, Written Early in the American Revolution
Tune—The Gods of Greece

In a chariot of light, from the regions of day,
The Goddess of Liberty came.
Ten thousand celestials directed her way,
And hither conducted the dame.
A fair budding branch from the gardens above,
Where millions with millions agree,
She brought in her hand as a pledge of her love,
And the plant she named Liberty Tree.

The celestial exotic stuck deep in the ground,
Like a native it flourished and bore;
The fame of its fruit drew the nations around
To seek out this peaceable shore.
Unmindful of names or distinctions they came,
For freemen like brothers agree;
With one spirit endued, they one friendship pursued,
And their temple was Liberty Tree.

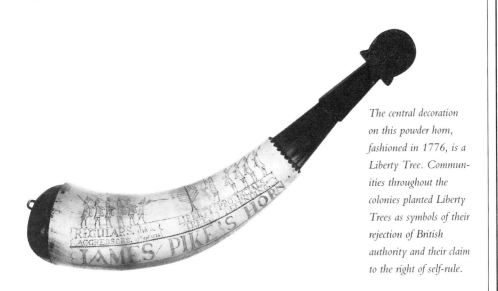

The central decoration on this powder horn, fashioned in 1776, is a Liberty Tree. Communities throughout the colonies planted Liberty Trees as symbols of their rejection of British authority and their claim to the right of self-rule.

Beneath this fair tree, like the patriarchs of old,
Their bread in contentment they ate,
Unvexed with the troubles of silver or gold,
The cares of the grand and the great.
With timber and tar they Old England supplied,
And supported her power on the sea:
Her battles they fought, without getting a groat,
For the honour of Liberty Tree.

But hear, O' ye swains ('tis a tale most profane),
How all the tyrannical powers,
Kings, Commons, and Lords, are uniting amain
To cut down this guardian of ours.
From the East to the West blow the trumpet to arms,
Thro' the land let the sound of it flee:
Let the far and the near all unite with a cheer,
In defence of our Liberty Tree.

song he composed in 1775, "The Liberty Tree," he aligned himself with the American cause.

Yet what exactly was America's cause? The restoration of "Englishmen's rights?" The reform of the imperial system? Or outright separation? Radicals such as Samuel Adams, John Adams, and the Virginian Thomas Jefferson privately discussed separation, but publicly they merely proposed reorganizing America's colonial relationship to Britain. And even though the colonials were sorely antagonized, the traditional attachment to the monarchy was so strong that many people regarded even this limited change as too extreme.

The *Pennsylvania Magazine* prospered under Paine's editorship, becoming the best-selling magazine in America. Nevertheless, Paine's relations with Witherspoon and Aitken had soured by the summer of 1775. Witherspoon turned against Paine for having the audacity to actually edit Witherspoon's words. In revenge, Witherspoon spread rumors that Paine drank heavily, a slur that would follow Paine to the grave. He did drink, mostly wine and brandy, but not at all to the extent his enemies claimed. Salary questions divided Paine and Aitken. Receiving a modest £50 per year, Paine, increasingly confident of his literary abilities, requested a raise. Aitken refused. By autumn Paine had left the magazine.

Paine did not withdraw simply because he was fed up. More important, he had decided upon a new, politically bold project—to write a pamphlet calling for separation from Britain.

A state of war between Britain and the American colonies already existed, ever since the Battles of Lexington and Concord in April 1775. In May 1775, the Second Continental Congress had convened in Philadelphia and created a Continental Army under the command of Virginia's George Washington. Still, peace overtures continued, and American goals remained undefined.

A number of people arose to debate the direction and meaning of the rebellion; but it was the newcomer, Paine, who would revolutionize American thinking.

Paine's writings had begun to garner significant attention, and he had been befriended by one of Congress's more radical members, the young Philadelphia doctor Benjamin Rush. When Paine told him of his plans, Rush counseled moderation, fearing that the time was not yet right. However, Paine would not be deterred. He was absolutely convinced that, although Americans did not speak openly of it, they yearned for independence. Whatever his reservations, Rush welcomed Paine's commitment, and in turn, Paine regularly sought his friend's editorial advice.

Starting in September, Paine devoted his energies to writing the pamphlet. History beckoned, and he could not afford to hesitate. Determined to reach the broadest possible audience, he held nothing back. He summoned forth his memories of Britain and his affections for America. He drew upon his readings in 18th-century liberal and republican political thought—readings that emphasized individual freedom and contended that individuals should create representative governments to protect their rights to life, liberty, and property—and he articulated those ideas with his understanding of popular, democratic political aspirations. Paine quoted the Bible, cited historical examples, and called upon the force of "reason" itself.

After completing the manuscript in December, he sent copies to Samuel Adams and Benjamin Franklin for their consideration. They liked it and suggested only minor revisions. Rush then introduced Paine to the Philadelphia publisher Robert Bell, who, sympathetic to the work's arguments, accepted the commission to print it. Paine had entitled his pamphlet *Plain Truth,* but Rush proposed another title, *Common Sense,* and Paine agreed.

On January 10, 1776, *Common Sense* swept onto the American scene and into American consciousness. In just two weeks the first printing sold out. Soon, supply could not keep

A state of war already prevailed between Britain and its American colonies when Paine's Common Sense *inspired Americans to turn their rebellion into revolution in 1776.*

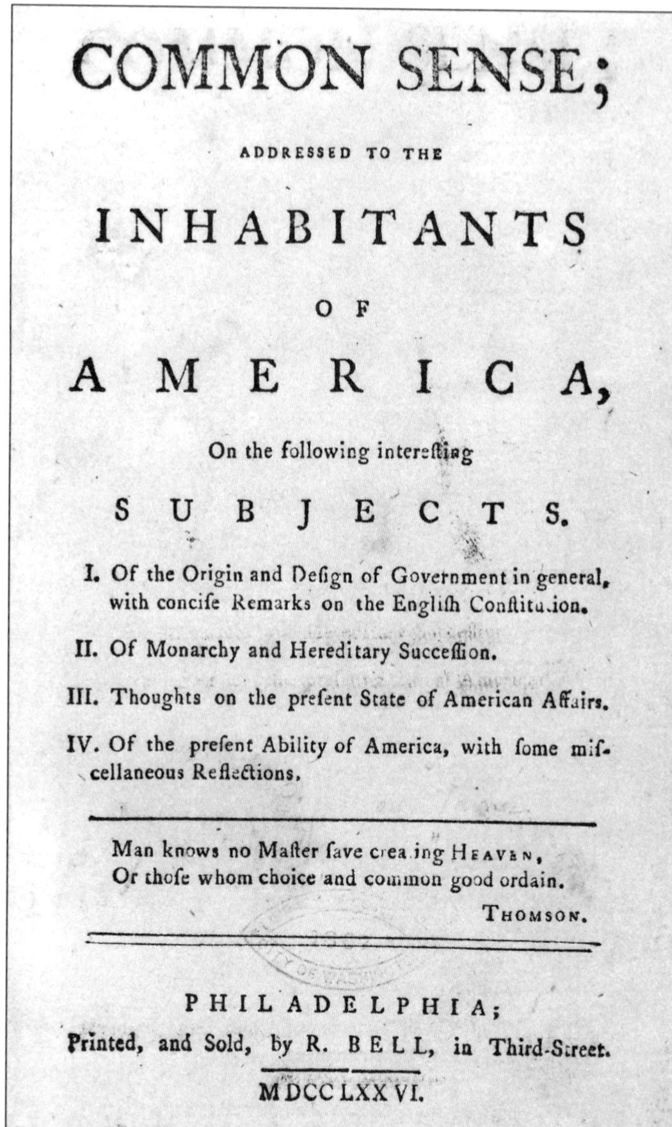

COMMON SENSE;

ADDRESSED TO THE

INHABITANTS

OF

AMERICA,

On the following intereſting

SUBJECTS.

I. Of the Origin and Deſign of Government in general, with conciſe Remarks on the Engliſh Conſtitution.

II. Of Monarchy and Hereditary Succeſſion.

III. Thoughts on the preſent State of American Affairs.

IV. Of the preſent Ability of America, with ſome miſcellaneous Reflections.

Man knows no Maſter ſave creating HEAVEN,
Or thoſe whom choice and common good ordain.

THOMSON.

PHILADELPHIA;
Printed, and Sold, by R. BELL, in Third-Street.
MDCCLXXVI.

up with demand. With or without permission, printing presses around the colonies issued new editions, including one in German for immigrants. During the next few months 150,000 copies were distributed in America alone (the equivalent today would be 15 million, making *Common Sense,* proportionally, the nation's greatest best-seller ever). And in very little time translations appeared in Europe.

Paine originally signed his pamphlet "Written by an Englishman." However, within weeks his authorship became known. He relished the attention it garnered him, but he sought no material rewards. Testifying to his dedication to the cause, he declined all royalties, insisting that any profits due him be used to purchase mittens for Washington's troops.

Common Sense transformed the colonial rebellion into a war for independence. And that was not all. Calling upon Americans to recognize their historical possibilities and responsibilities and make a true revolution of their struggles, Paine harnessed their shared (but as yet unstated) thoughts and expressed them in language bold and clear. He forcefully declared the American cause to be more than a question of separation from Britain. Announcing that "[t]he sun never shined on a cause of greater worth," he proclaimed it a campaign against the tyranny of hereditary privilege both "monarchical and aristocratical" and for a democratic republic.

Even before issuing the call for independence, Paine dealt with Americans' surviving attachments to king, empire, and Britain. He knew that most Americans were still trapped within the confines of the old constitutional argument between Britain and the colonies. He also knew that that there was only one part of that connection that Americans still cherished—their allegiance to the monarchy. He realized that if he could slash through that last link, he would explode the whole constitutional context of the argument and make way for a new argument, one about independence, one that would command Americans' attention, respect, and, ultimately, allegiance.

Paine admitted that English kings were no longer absolute monarchs, but—taking issue with those who credited the benevolence of the British constitution for this—he wrote that "*it is wholly owing to the constitution of the people, and not to the constitution of the government* that the crown is not as oppressive in England as in Turkey." Paine argued that the British monarchy was a ridiculous institution whose origins were certainly not ordained by God:

> A French bastard [William the Conqueror] landing with an armed banditti, and establishing himself king of England against the consent of the natives, is in plain terms a very paltry rascally original.—It certainly hath no divinity in it.... The plain truth is, that the antiquity of English monarchy will not bear looking into.

Appealing to Americans' religious and egalitarian sentiments, he added that "hereditary succession" compounds the evil of monarchy: "For all men being originally equals, no *one* by *birth* could have a right to set up his own family in perpetual preference to all others for ever." He humorously observed, "One of the strongest *natural* proofs of the folly of hereditary right in kings, is, that nature disapproves it, otherwise she would not so frequently turn it into ridicule by giving mankind an *ass for a lion*." And, pointing to England's own history, he charged that "monarchy and succession have laid (not this or that kingdom only) but the world in blood and ashes."

As for Britain being America's "parent country," Paine utterly rejected the proposition. He described Britain's conduct as selfish and shameful: "Even brutes do not devour their young, nor savages make war upon their families." If anything, he argued, "Europe, not England, is the parent country of America. This new world hath been the asylum for the persecuted lovers of civil and religious liberty from *every part* of Europe.... [w]e claim brotherhood with every European Christian."

Paine then turned to America. He appealed directly to Americans' economic interests. In addition to outlining the tremendous commercial prospects that would follow liberation from British imperialism, he offered a vision of independence that asked his readers to see themselves as *Americans*, a people no longer subject to king and nobility but—as was their "natural right"—free and equal before God and "the law" and governing themselves through democratically elected representatives.

Urging unity, Paine portrayed America not as 13 separate entities but as a nation-state: "Now is the seed time of continental union, faith and honour. . . ." Our strength is continental not provincial." Proposing a republican form of government, he recommended a one-chamber Continental Congress headed by a rotating President. Finally, he surveyed America's physical and material riches to prove it had the resources to actually accomplish the revolution.

Philosophers have argued about the originality of Paine's ideas. But one thing is certain: They were radically original in appeal and consequence. Elite colonial intellectuals had penned many a speech and pamphlet, but they had narrowly addressed themselves to the property-owning classes. Paine—artisan by upbringing and intellectual by effort—addressed himself to Americans of all classes (of white society). The very style and content of his words entailed a more democratic conception of "the people" than had prevailed up to that time. Paine wrote not only so working people could understand, but also to integrate them into the political community. Capturing the imagination of mechanics and farmers in an unprecedented fashion, he recruited them to the cause of independence and further empowered them to restructure the political and social order. He devised a new way of arguing about politics and a more democratic language of politics than ever before existed.

Paine failed to incorporate either his abolitionist views or his concerns about the status of women into *Common Sense*. However, praising America's religious diversity, he connected the advance of religious freedom to the cause of independence and the creation of a new polity. America would serve as a model to the world and, welcoming immigrants, as a refuge:

> O ye that love mankind! Ye that dare oppose, not only tyranny, but the tyrant, stand forth! Every spot of the world is over-run with oppression. Freedom hath been hunted round the globe. Asia and Africa have long expelled her.—Europe regards her like a stranger, and England hath given her warning to depart. O! receive the fugitive, and prepare in time an asylum for mankind.

Paine's vision of a democratic republic was potentially unlimited. This point was well understood, and it aroused a strong reaction in some circles. Loyalist Tories, who desired reconciliation with England, vehemently denounced *Common Sense* and its author. At the same time, socially prominent patriots such as John Adams, though pleased by Paine's call for independence, criticized him and his ideas because they feared the radical, popular, and democratic aspirations his pamphlet evoked.

For Paine, the American Revolution possessed world-historical importance: "[P]osterity are virtually involved in the contest, and will be more or less affected, even to the end of time, by the proceedings now.... The cause of America is in a great measure the cause of all mankind." Indeed, whereas before this time "revolution" meant merely the act of revolving, like a planet in its orbit, hereafter it meant to overthrow an old regime and create a new one.

Weeks passed before anyone in the Continental Congress responded openly to the arguments in *Common Sense.* Apparently, the delegates did not know what to do. But it created a great commotion in other places. In Virginia, Edmund Randolph observed that it "insinuated itself into the hearts of the people." In Massachusetts, Deacon Palmer stated, "I believe no pages were ever more eagerly read, nor more generally approved. People speak of it in rapturous praise." George Washington, already in the field commanding the Continental Army, reported that Paine's pamphlet was "working a wonderful change in the minds of many men," adding that his own reading of it had finally persuaded him of the need to break with Britain.

Reservations persisted, however. Elites feared the new popular politics of the working classes, but most figured they would be better trying to lead than resist it. In the spring, assemblies began to issue resolutions calling for independence and instructing their delegates at Philadelphia to follow suit. Finally, in June, Congress appointed a committee headed by Thomas Jefferson to draft an American Declaration of Independence. Paine was not a member of the committee, but all the members had read his *Common Sense*.

On the cap of this American rifleman, a skull and crossbones and the words "or liberty" portray one of the most popular slogans of the day, "Liberty or Death." The initials "CC" on the ammunition pouch designate a soldier in the service of the Continental Congress.

CHAPTER

5

Revolutionary War

On July 4, 1776, the United States of America declared its independence. Yet several more years of war would have to be endured to secure that independence, and during this time Americans would face many a challenge and be tested severely. Paine himself would serve the Patriots' cause in many ways—as soldier, war correspondent, government official, diplomat—but he would continue to make his most important contributions as a revolutionary pamphleteer.

Immediately following the Declaration of Independence, Paine enlisted in the military to serve as personal secretary to General Daniel Roberdeau, commander of the Associators. Filled with short-term recruits, the Associators were to operate as a "flying camp"—so named because the task of such units was to rush, as swiftly as a flight of birds, to where they were needed at the front lines.

Within days of Paine's arrival, the Associators were marching toward New York, where George Washington's 19,000 relatively inexperienced American troops awaited the British. Taking up a position at Perth Amboy, New Jersey, Paine and his comrades witnessed the British fleet's arrival at Staten Island. The sight of the 73 ships, 13,000 sailors, and 32,000 well-equipped soldiers chilled the Americans, and Roberdeau and Paine had to work hard to prevent desertions.

In September, at the end of the enlistment period, the camp broke up without having seen any action. Most of the men returned to Philadelphia. But Paine went North to join the Continental Army as aide to General Nathanael Greene, commander of the American forces on the Hudson River at Fort Lee and Fort Washington. From the palisades on the New Jersey side of the river, Paine could take in all of New York, allowing him to follow Washington's engagements against the British, who were led by General Sir William Howe.

Along with gathering intelligence for Greene, Paine provided accounts of the situation for Philadelphia's newspapers. While reporting the facts, he made every effort to instill hope in his readers. But the situation went from bad to awful. By November, Washington's army had been beaten harshly and had to withdraw from New York. Pursued by the British, Washington soon ordered a total retreat South through New Jersey. Finally, crossing the Delaware River in December, the Continental Army halted on the Pennsylvania side. Though it seemed the revolution was about to be crushed, Paine refused to tolerate such thinking. Throughout the march he continued to send reports back to Philadelphia, describing the retreat as a strategic maneuver.

Discouragement and defeatism spread. Paine decided to compose a new revolutionary pamphlet. But to do this he needed to return to Philadelphia. With permission, he separated from the army at Trenton, and made his way across the next 33 miles alone and on foot, sleeping and eating when and where he could. What he discovered on arrival confirmed his worst fears. Expecting the British to take and sack the city, the Congress had departed for Baltimore, and panicked residents were hurriedly packing up to follow its example. The remaining Tories were preparing a welcome for the British.

Less than a year earlier, Paine had inspired his fellow citizens-to-be to recognize their shared aspirations and make history. He knew they urgently needed to be inspired anew, so he quickly set himself to writing the new pamphlet, which he called *The American Crisis.* His opening words would resound through the generations:

> These are the times that try men's souls: The summer soldier and the sunshine patriot will, in this crisis, shrink from the service of their country; but he that stands it now, deserves the love and thanks of man and woman. Tyranny, like hell, is not easily conquered; yet we have this consolation with us, that the harder the conflict, the more glorious the triumph. What we obtain too cheap, we esteem too lightly—'Tis dearness only that gives everything its value.

Paine went on to ridicule King George III, attack the Loyalists, praise the success of Washington's retreat, and—reassuring Americans that they were up to repulsing it—warn of the British advance on Philadelphia. He closed by restating Americans' choices, perseverance or submission—the former ensuring victory and independence, the latter, defeat and servitude.

The American Crisis appeared on December 19, 1776, in a first printing of 18,000. Again, Paine relinquished any claim to royalties. As before, tens of thousands of copies, both licensed and pirated, were sold—and in the late 18th century such writings would as often be read aloud to gatherings as alone in private. Paine himself revealed a remarkable awareness of his task and talents as an intellectual serving not the elite but the people: "I dwell not upon vapours of the imagination; I bring reason to your ears; and in language, as plain as A, B, C, hold up truth to your eyes."

The pamphlet would be the first of 13 Crisis Papers Paine was to write during the course of the war. They

With George Washington's army in retreat and America's cause in jeopardy, Paine wrote his first American Crisis *paper in December 1776 to encourage his fellow Americans to renew their commitment to the struggle for independence.*

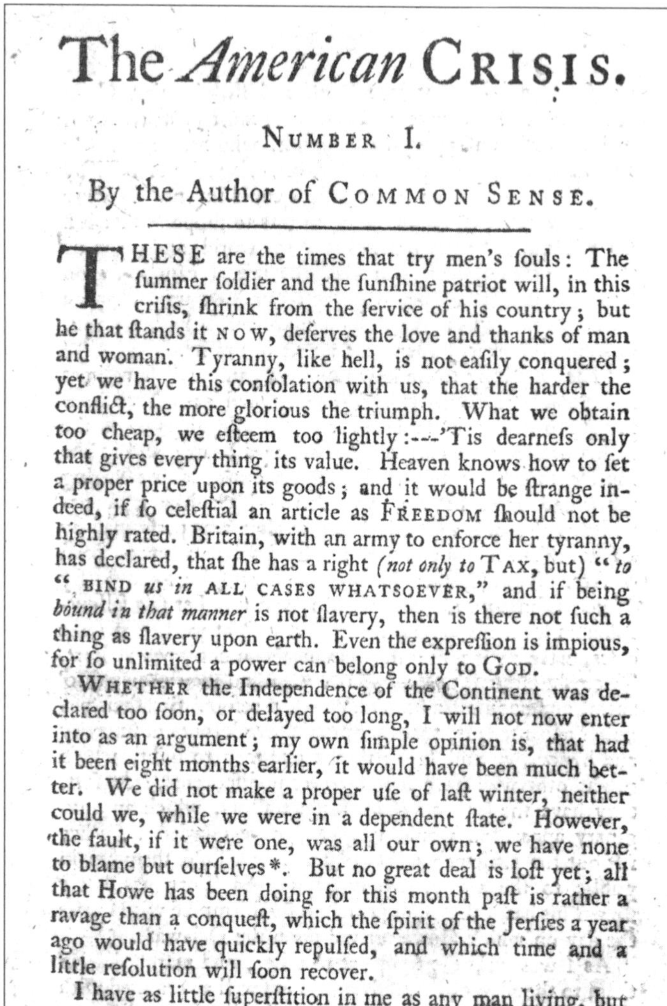

The *American* CRISIS.

NUMBER I.

By the Author of COMMON SENSE.

THESE are the times that try men's ſouls: The ſummer ſoldier and the ſunſhine patriot will, in this criſis, ſhrink from the ſervice of his country; but he that ſtands it NOW, deſerves the love and thanks of man and woman. Tyranny, like hell, is not eaſily conquered; yet we have this conſolation with us, that the harder the conflict, the more glorious the triumph. What we obtain too cheap, we eſteem too lightly:---'Tis dearneſs only that gives every thing its value. Heaven knows how to ſet a proper price upon its goods; and it would be ſtrange indeed, if ſo celeſtial an article as FREEDOM ſhould not be highly rated. Britain, with an army to enforce her tyranny, has declared, that ſhe has a right *(not only to* TAX, but) "*to* "BIND *us in* ALL CASES WHATSOEVER," and if being *bound in that manner* is not ſlavery, then is there not ſuch a thing as ſlavery upon earth. Even the expreſſion is impious, for ſo unlimited a power can belong only to GOD.

WHETHER the Independence of the Continent was declared too ſoon, or delayed too long, I will not now enter into as an argument; my own ſimple opinion is, that had it been eight months earlier, it would have been much better. We did not make a proper uſe of laſt winter, neither could we, while we were in a dependent ſtate. However, the fault, if it were one, was all our own; we have none to blame but ourſelves*. But no great deal is loſt yet; all that Howe has been doing for this month paſt is rather a ravage than a conqueſt, which the ſpirit of the Jerſies a year ago would have quickly repulſed, and which time and a little reſolution will ſoon recover.

I have as little ſuperſtition in me as any man living, but

proved invaluable to the Patriot cause, but none more so, perhaps, than the first.

In desperate need of a victory, Washington decided to stage a Christmas Night attack on the British forces—mostly Hessian mercenaries from Germany, hired foreign troops occupying Trenton. The story is told that before boarding the boats to recross the Delaware's icy and treacherous waters, Washington's officers gathered the men together and read them passages from *The American Crisis*. That night they caught the Hessian garrison completely by surprise.

Washington then speedily struck at British forces at Princeton. The United States had secured its first genuine triumphs of the war.

In mid-January, Paine published a second Crisis Paper, presented in the form of a defiant open letter to the British commander, General Howe. A few days later, the Pennsylvania Council of Safety invited Paine to serve as secretary to a joint state and Congressional delegation seeking to negotiate an alliance with several tribes of the Iroquois. Meeting at Easton with a delegation of chiefs, Paine was greatly impressed by the Native Americans' dignity, reason, and intelligence. Though the negotiators reached an agreement, Congress later rejected it, claiming that the Indians had pretended to negotiate on behalf of the whole Iroquois Confederacy although most of the Iroquois were already aligned with the British. The American revolutionaries did find Indian allies, but they regularly described Indian peoples as "savages." Paine, on the other hand—admiring the Native Americans' love of liberty and spirit of resistance—called them his "brothers."

On his return to Philadelphia in February, Paine, now 40 years old, became embroiled in the debate over Pennsylvania's proposed state constitution. Influenced by *Common Sense* and responding to the aspirations of the working classes, radicals had authored a document providing for a one-house legislature and the right to vote for all taxpaying men, making this the most democratic of the original state constitutions. Conservatives such as Robert Morris, a financier, and Matthew Slough, a wealthy manufacturer, adamantly opposed the constitution, fearful of the right to vote for propertyless workingmen and of the omission of the principles of separation of powers and checks and balances within government. Given the need for wartime unity, Paine tried at first to avoid conflict. But he naturally sided with the radicals, and in March, in order to defend the new constitution, he helped organize the Whig

Society (the name of which referred back to the group of prominent late-17th-century English radicals and reformers who opposed the power of the English crown).

That same month, Congress returned to Philadelphia. Its business included creating a Committee for Foreign Affairs. Though he had been a critic of Paine's kind of democratic radicalism, John Adams graciously nominated Paine to be the committee's paid secretary and—except for opposition by John Witherspoon, Paine's antagonist from the days of the *Pennsylvania Magazine*—he was roundly supported. Honored and elated, Paine accepted the appointment and swore the required oath of secrecy (the post made him responsible for the Committee's secret files and correspondence). He worked hard and enjoyed the salary and status the position afforded; indeed, allowing his new sense of importance to get the better of him, Paine occasionally referred to himself as Secretary for Foreign Affairs.

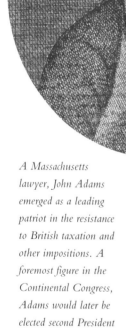

A Massachusetts lawyer, John Adams emerged as a leading patriot in the resistance to British taxation and other impositions. A foremost figure in the Continental Congress, Adams would later be elected second President of the United States.

Only days following his appointment, Paine's third Crisis Paper appeared. In it he vehemently attacked the Tories and proposed that all Americans take a loyalty oath, moderately adding that a high property tax be levied against those who refused. Loyalists did suffer at Patriots' hands in the course of the revolutionary war, and up to 100,000 Tories fled the country; but Americans were comparatively lenient with the counterrevolutionaries in their midst.

Meanwhile, the British continued to threaten. In July, Paine wrote to Franklin saying that he and David

Rittenhouse, a well-known radical, watchmaker, and scientist, were experimenting with a bow capable of shooting flaming steel-tipped arrows across the Delaware. He included in his letter a sketch of the envisioned bow and arrow, but he and Rittenhouse never completed the project, for in late August, things turned ugly. British forces, commanded by General Charles Cornwallis, landed along the Delaware Bay and advanced on Philadelphia. Washington's army fell back after suffering severe losses. Philadelphians once again prepared to abandon their city, and Paine tried to rally them in a fourth Crisis Paper:

> Men who are sincere in defending their freedom, will always feel concern at every circumstance, which seems to make against them.... But the dejection lasts only for a moment; they soon rise out of it with additional vigor; the glow of hope, courage and fortitude, will, in a little time, supply the place of every inferior passion, and kindle the whole heart into heroism.

Nevertheless, fearing the worst, one-third of the city's residents left by mid-September. Congress, too, packed up and headed west to York, Pennsylvania. Paine stayed on to the last moment; however, on September 19, with the British occupying the city, he escaped to Trenton with the Committee's records.

Paine first took refuge at the home of his friend Colonel Joseph Kirkbride, near Bordentown, New Jersey. He next found his way to Washington's headquarters north of Philadelphia. The picture looked bleak; the army was in appalling shape. Then grand news came from upstate New York that a Patriot army under General Horatio Gates had defeated the British under the command of General John "Gentleman Johnny" Burgoyne at the Battle of Saratoga. The victory did not alter Washington's immediate plight, but it definitely represented a turning point in the war.

The battle's outcome meant that the strategic Hudson Valley would remain in American control. Moreover, when

In the winter of 1777–78, George Washington and his ragged army encamped at Valley Forge, Pennsylvania. Rumors spread that Congress would replace Washington in view of his recent military setbacks. Here, Washington meets with the Committee of Congress at Valley Forge to determine a course of action.

word reached Paris, the news induced France to officially recognize the independence of the United States and, soon after, to enter into a wartime alliance with the new nation.

That winter, 1777–78, Washington encamped his weakened army at Valley Forge, where severe cold and heavy snow further battered the U.S. troops. Paine, following another brief military stint with General Greene, went west to Lancaster, Pennsylvania, where he spent the winter months with the gunsmith William Henry and his family. After a series of arduous journeys, Paine slept long hours and enjoyed their hospitality. He also penned the fifth Crisis Paper, berating General Howe, now in control of Philadelphia, and praising Washington, whose leadership some had begun to question.

Though his army emerged from Valley Forge in its worst shape ever, Washington remained in command, and following their defeat at Saratoga, the British made no further attempt to subdue the northern states. In the summer of 1778, the latter would evacuate Philadelphia in order to regroup in New York City and shift their efforts south, believing the greater number of Loyalists in those states would rush to support them.

Meanwhile, Paine got himself entangled—and in very deep trouble—in the Silas Deane affair. Deane, a lawyer, merchant, and Connecticut Congressional delegate, had received a secret commission from Congress early in the war to go to Paris in pursuit of French financial and material aid. Congress rightly assumed that Britain's enemy would be interested in befriending the rebellious colonies, and in fact, France secretly began to help the U.S. cause soon after the Declaration of Independence. But naturally, the French government insisted that its assistance not be revealed, and until recognition and the formal alliance following the Battle of Saratoga, that remained the case.

After a couple of years, members of Congress began to grow suspicious of Deane's dealings, especially when certain arms shipments he had arranged arrived with an overly high price tag.

Believing that Deane was engaging in corruption and war profiteering, Congress recalled him from France in late 1777 so that he could testify at secret Congressional hearings. However, eager to proclaim his innocence and halt the spread of scandalous rumors, Deane openly defended his actions in the press.

As secretary to the Committee for Foreign Affairs, Paine himself had played something of a role in securing French aid, and his post gave him access to the secret correspondence between the United States and France. His reading of the files convinced him of Deane's corruption, and his outrage grew with Deane's claims of innocence, all the more because Deane had gone into print with them. Without consulting the Committee for Foreign Affairs,

Paine rushed to reply to Deane in the press. Though he acted from principle, he committed a terrible blunder, badly embarrassing the French and U.S. governments. In making use of secret correspondence to challenge Deane's assertions, Paine publicly revealed France's previously hidden support, and the revelations were made just as the new French ambassador was arriving in America.

Paine's actions blew up in his face. Deane had rich and powerful friends in Congress, such as the financier Robert Morris and the lawyer Gouverneur Morris (the two were unrelated), who had already taken a dislike to Paine following the conflicts over Pennsylvania's constitution. They now exerted all their influence against him. They made Paine's own behavior and character an issue in the case: Had he not breached his sworn oath of secrecy? Becoming ever more heated, the controversy persisted for the following year—and its memory was to dog Paine for some time to come.

To some extent, history would ultimately absolve Paine. Deane later turned out to be not only a cheat, a thief, and a liar, but also a supporter of the British monarchy and a traitor to his country. Yet, as much as Paine tried, he could not prevail against the forces arrayed against him in Congress at the time. After a series of nasty confrontations, harried by his political enemies, he felt compelled to resign his post in January 1779. Public insults followed him. Convinced he had done the right thing, Paine replied to his attackers. But he got nowhere.

In July 1779, Paine's friends rallied to support him in a public gathering. He appreciated the gesture, but he really needed work and an income. To his credit, he did pass up one potentially lucrative invitation. Strangely, right after his resignation as secretary to the Foreign Affairs Committee, the French government tried to hire him to write propaganda promoting the Franco-American alliance. However, unwilling to subject his pen to ends to which he did not feel strongly committed, Paine refused the offer. Rather, he accepted a temporary, low-paying clerk's job with Owen Biddle, a Philadelphia Quaker and grain merchant.

In late summer, a debilitating fever struck Paine, sending him to bed for several weeks. Friends tended to his needs, but on recovery he still faced unemployment and poverty. Paine's allies remembered his role in Pennsylvania's constitutional debates and, luckily, they were able to rescue him with appointment as clerk to the Pennsylvania Assembly. In the new post, Paine helped in authoring the preamble to legislation abolishing slavery in the state, the first measure of its kind in the United States. Disappointing Paine and other abolitionists, the law itself did not immediately emancipate the slaves, but it did provide for slavery's eventual end in Pennsylvania by declaring that at age 28 the children of slaves were to be freed.

The geographic focus of the war had shifted, but the struggle for independence raged on, and in 1780 Paine issued fresh Crisis Papers and a few related pieces. The U.S. defeat at Charleston, South Carolina, and Benedict Arnold's treasonous actions at West Point, New York—Arnold offered to turn the fort over to British forces in exchange for money and a high-ranking commission in the British army—compelled Paine to write. In particular, he addressed the need for more men and material for the war effort. To pay for the added soldiers and supplies, Paine proposed that wealthy citizens advance the necessary funds, and to set a good example, he donated $500 of his own money (a sizable sum, especially for Paine, who was not affluent). The funds collected served as the foundation for the first bank in the United States, the Bank of Pennsylvania, later chartered by Congress as the Bank of North America.

Paine had returned to the political fray and, now that he was no longer driven to constantly defend himself, his spirits revived. Adding to his renewed sense of respect, on July 4, 1780, the University of Pennsylvania awarded him an honorary master of arts degree. He enjoyed the recognition, but he did not boast of it.

Paine's politics were clearly democratic. At the same time, he was also persuaded that the survival of the United States, and its future ability to project republican democracy as a model for the world, required the development of a stronger national government than that afforded by the Articles of Confederation—the first written framework of government for the United States, which had been approved by Congress in 1777 but had not yet been ratified by all the states.

A dispute among the states over the future of the western territories substantiated Paine's concerns. The Articles clearly deferred on the issue to those states, like Virginia, that held expansionary claims to western lands, leading a locked-in state like Maryland to resist ratification. Paine intervened with a special pamphlet, *Public Good*, arguing that the territories should be treated as federal property, to be settled by Americans and eventually admitted as new states. He concluded by recommending that a continental convention be convened in order to create a new, more effective Constitution. Such a convention remained several years away (1787), but well before then states with claims on western territory began to drop most of their claims, and Maryland ratified the Articles.

In October 1780, prior to publishing *Public Good*, Paine wrote *The Crisis Extraordinary*, in which he linked the questions of national unity and national finance. Commencing with an estimate of the pressing needs of the federal government, Paine advocated that Congress be granted the authority to levy taxes directly. Doubtful he could get Americans to readily agree, he proceeded to suggest that they seek more funds from the French. He followed up on this by writing directly to France's Foreign Minister, the Comte de Vergennes, sending a copy to Ralph Izard, a South Carolina congressman.

Paine's letter coaxed Congress to approach its French ally for increased support. Late in 1780, Congress empowered young Colonel John Laurens, an aide to Washington, to travel to France and present the U.S. case with the assistance of Benjamin Franklin (already in Paris representing the United States). Having met Paine a few years earlier at Washington's headquarters, and trusting his thinking on political and financial matters, Laurens requested that Congress assign Paine to his mission. Paine himself thought the idea splendid, for he had been concocting schemes about directing propaganda against Britain from a much closer vantage point, such as France or, more outrageously, in disguise from within England itself. However, Paine's enemies aggressively blocked his appointment.

Insulted, Paine nevertheless resolved to accompany Laurens in an unofficial capacity and at his own expense. Knowing he could well use Paine's advice in dealing with the French (though Paine did not speak the language), Laurens welcomed him along. After paying a visit to Washington's headquarters in New Jersey, Laurens and Paine traveled to Boston to board the gunboat *Alliance* whose commander, Captain John Barry, was renowned for successful actions against the British. On the evening of February 11, 1781, they sailed for France.

Paine's original voyage to America had almost killed him. It seemed for a while that his return across the Atlantic would finish the job. Less than a week out of Boston, sailing south of Newfoundland, the *Alliance* ran into icebergs and rough weather. Wind tore at the sails, and ice floes smashed against the ship's sides. Paine would later write: "The sea, in whatever direction it could be seen, appeared a tumultuous assemblage of floating rolling rocks, which we could not avoid and against which there was no defense." Fortunately, after several nightmarish hours they escaped the floes and the winds died down. Captain Barry ordered that repairs be made en route.

Winter's worst did not show itself again. Yet there were further adventures ahead. South of Greenland they came upon a pair of enemy ships. Barry pursued them, ordering all on board the *Alliance* to prepare for battle. However, when the two ships turned about to take up the challenge, Barry intelligently decided to withdraw. The next day, the *Alliance* encountered a Scottish ship, the *Russel*, in possession of a heavily laden Venetian ship. The *Russel* turned its prize loose and fled. Barry and his men, including Laurens and Paine, boarded the Venetian ship and found its captain and crew in irons. According to the rules of privateering (which Paine knew well), Barry and his crew could now claim the prize. However, determining that the Venetians had been captured in an act of piracy, Barry set them free—making Paine exceedingly proud to be sailing as an American. The *Alliance* also engaged and captured a British gunboat, the *Alert*, in the course of which action Paine is said to have dueled with the *Alert*'s captain, the Comte de Noailles.

In spite of everything, Barry made the voyage in near-record time, bringing the *Alliance* into port at L'Orient in Brittany on March 9, 1781. A large crowd welcomed them. Paine himself was treated as something of a celebrity, which pleased him greatly. Several of the dignitaries later remarked that though they found Paine's manner eccentric, they enjoyed his openness and enthusiasm for ideas.

Laurens and Paine journeyed separately to Paris, for Paine received an invitation to go first to Nantes. They later rendezvoused in the French capital, where they met up with Franklin. Paine, as promised, served as Laurens's secretary, avidly maintaining correspondence and filing regular reports. Laurens himself got off to a bad start; however, with Franklin's and Paine's assistance, he ended up acquitting himself well and succeeded in securing a sizable grant from the French.

Mission accomplished, on June 1 Laurens and Paine boarded the French frigate *La Résolute* at Brest and sailed

New York harbor as it appeared in the 1770s. The port cities of Boston, New York, Philadelphia, and Charleston had become important cultural and commercial centers by the 1760s, attracting the traffic of boats and ships.

for Philadelphia in convoy with several other ships. Carrying cash and supplies for the American war effort, they went out of their way to avoid confrontations with the enemy, and learning of British warships in the Delaware Bay, they changed their destination. Finally, they landed in Boston on August 26.

Congress applauded Laurens for his diplomatic accomplishments. Paine, however, received neither official thanks nor public recognition, and he resented it. He had spent all his savings on the trip and had worked hard for the Patriots' cause. Returning to Philadelphia, he once again stared at unemployment and destitution.

On October 19, 1781, British general Charles Cornwallis surrendered to George Washington at Yorktown, Virginia, effectively ending the Revolutionary War; however, the Treaty of Paris between Britain and the United States was not signed until September 4, 1783.

CHAPTER

6

PEACE

On October 19, 1781, at Yorktown, Virginia, American forces defeated the British under the command of General Lord Charles Cornwallis. Eighteen months would pass before peace would officially be achieved, but Yorktown proved to be the last major battle of the war.

Soon Americans would have to begin to confront the challenges of independent nationhood and address the injustices and inequalities that had existed throughout their history. Struggles would ensue, and changes would be made. Certain contradictions and conflicts would persist, and new ones would arise. Yet the ideals of liberty, equality, and democracy—ideas that Tom Paine helped to cultivate and Thomas Jefferson and the Founding Fathers inscribed in the Declaration of Independence—would forever shape the development of the United States. Paine himself would continue to write in favor of creating a new nation-state, but the advent of peace would also permit him to take up older interests, at least for a while.

In the autumn of 1781, Paine was broke. He never expected wealth from his revolutionary labors, but, always believing in America's chances, neither did he expect to suffer penury. He wrote to George Washington, hoping that the general could secure him some compensation and, possibly, a new appointment. Appreciative of Paine's contributions, Washington succeeded in rounding up some money for him. Washington also sent a letter to Robert Morris, one of Paine's old antagonists, suggesting that Morris and his associates secretly employ Paine's literary skills to promote national unity and the interests of the federal government.

Morris and Paine met occasionally through the fall and, in February 1782, worked out an agreement whereby Paine would write newspaper columns and pamphlets, including further installments of the Crisis Papers, and receive $800 yearly to be covered by Morris, Washington, and Robert Livingston, the newly appointed secretary of foreign affairs. Additionally, Washington helped arrange for Paine to write for the French government. Making it clear to all parties that he would write nothing with which he did not agree, he enthusiastically took up the commissions.

For several years, Paine had hoped to write a history of the Revolution. Though he would never get around to it, he did render a valuable critical interpretation of its history. Morris had loaned him a copy of *The Revolution of America* by the abbot Guillaume Raynal, a distinguished French writer and political thinker. Raynal contended that the Revolution differed very little from rebellions in the past. Maintaining that tax questions alone had instigated events, he rejected the idea that political principles had motivated Americans. Paine could not allow such claims to go unanswered. In the summer of 1782, he responded in the pamphlet *Letter to the Abbé Raynal*. Correcting the abbot, he insisted on the Revolution's originality: "Here the value and quality of liberty, the nature of government, and the dignity of man, were known and understood, and the attachment of the Americans to these principles produced the Revolution, as a natural and almost unavoidable consequence."

Paine closed by repeating his assertion that the Revolution represented a development of global importance and, not for the first time, referred to himself as a "universal citizen." In this vein, it is often recounted that on hearing his dear old friend Ben Franklin declare, "Where liberty is, there is my country," Paine cried out in reply, "Where liberty is not, there is my country." In other words, even after the revolution for democracy and a republican government had been realized in America, the struggle would be far from over.

In the winter of 1782–83 Paine concerned himself with the matter of federal finances; in particular, he addressed Rhode Island's refusal to pay the taxes that Congress had mandated on goods imported to the United States. In what came to be called *Six Letters to Rhode Island*, he urged Rhode Islanders to appreciate the need for unity and to fulfill their obligations as citizens of the United States. The opposition saw the central government and its taxes as tools of the merchant elites and accused Paine of being nothing more than "a hired pen" (which he was, but he was not only that). Paine failed to change their minds.

In April 1783, an armistice ended the war (the Treaty of Paris would be signed in September). Paine wrote in the final Crisis Paper: "'The times that tried men souls' are over—and the greatest and compleatest [sic] revolution the world ever knew is gloriously and happily accomplished." In fact, Paine felt anxious. From the outset, he had never hesitated. He had given his greatest writings—the greatest political writings of their day—free to the cause. What would he do now, at 46 years of age? American independence was secured, but what of his own?

In June, no longer subsidized by Morris or the French, Paine desperately decided to petition Congress for financial support. He detailed his contributions to the creation of the United States. Congress took his request seriously but referred it to a committee. Paine then wrote another letter in which he offered to serve as official historian of the United States subsequent to receiving compensation for his earlier services. But when Congress offered the appointment without addressing his original request, he turned it down.

Still hoping for Congressional action, Paine used his remaining funds to buy a home in Bordentown near his old friends the Kirkbrides. While Congress hesitated, Paine's political allies pursued compensation for him in a number of state assemblies. Efforts failed in Virginia, but in the summer of 1784, New York endowed Paine with a 300-acre estate and farmhouse in New Rochelle, 30 miles northeast of New York City. A year later, Pennsylvania awarded him a small sum of money, and finally, in the autumn of 1785, Congress provided him with a grant of $3,000. Though Paine would never be rich, he would never again be impoverished in America.

In 1785 New York granted Paine this farmstead north of New York City. His cottage still stands on the property near present-day Paine Avenue in New Rochelle.

Renting out his Bordentown and New Rochelle properties, Paine moved to New York City, where he enjoyed an active social life during the first half of 1785. But by the autumn he was drawn back into public debate, this time around the question of the Bank of North America, the establishment of which he had helped foster. In the face of a deep postwar economic decline and growing indebtedness, especially among farmers, radical politicians called for the bank's charter to be withdrawn. They attributed the people's economic woes to the bank's concentration of financial power in the hands of an urban elite. Paine, however, ardently opposed terminating the bank, infuriating many of his friends and associates. They accused him of selling out to the mercantile and financial interests, who almost unanimously seemed to favor the bank's survival.

Paine's reasons for supporting the bank had nothing to do with selling out to the moneyed interests. He had always believed that America's future depended on national cohesion, sound fiscal policies, and the expansion of trade, commerce, and industry. To Paine, the bank's endeavors promoted those goals. Arguably, the bank question was not even a class question, but rather a matter of rural versus urban interests. Moreover, it was not so clear that Paine had abandoned the popular classes, for urban artisans themselves—the class with whom he is regularly identified—had split on the issue.

At the same time, the controversy did lead Paine to give up his earlier radical-democratic commitment to single-chamber legislatures. The antibank forces prevailed in the Pennsylvania Assembly and repealed the Bank of North America's charter. Paine comprehended the action as sad evidence of the unchecked rise of political parties and factions. This he thought dangerous. Factionalism, he believed, might lead to the triumph of a single faction, which might then lead to one-party rule and dictatorship. Naively holding to the idea that republican politics need

This sketch is based on Tom Paine's design for a cast-iron bridge. Builders near Sunderland, England, considered erecting it, but the bridge was never built.

not—and should not—degenerate into party politics and factional strife, Paine came out in support of bicameral (two-chamber) legislatures as a means of creating political balance and curbing such developments. To his satisfaction, the pro-bank forces handily won the Pennsylvania elections of 1786 and restored the bank's charter the following spring.

Paine had returned to Bordentown in September 1785, eager to commence work on a long-brewing project, the design and construction of an iron bridge. He had never stopped thinking about science and technology, and he had even undertaken a few experiments during and after the war. In the summer of 1777, he had worked with David Rittenhouse to try to create a bow capable of shooting giant flaming arrows across the Delaware at advancing British troops. In 1783, just after the signing of the peace treaty with Britain, he had visited George Washington in Princeton, New Jersey, and the two men had conducted a number of experiments, including setting fire to the surface of a nearby stream whose chemical properties fascinated them. Even as he was putting together his plans for the iron bridge, Paine spent a bit of time inventing "smokeless candles" that reportedly "greatly improved the light." But he did not market them. He now hoped to be able to devote himself to such pursuits.

People had often spoken of building a bridge over Pennsylvania's Schuylkill River, which flows into the Delaware at Philadelphia. But bridges at that time were still made of wood, and thus, they could not effectively endure the impact of winter ice. Not only did Paine conceive of an iron bridge. His design involved a single, long arch, instead of piers standing in midcurrent. With Franklin as a mentor, and assisted by the draftsman John Hall, Paine set to work constructing a model, completing it for display in Pennsylvania's State House on January 1, 1787.

Pennsylvanians were impressed with the 13-foot wrought-iron model (one foot for each state), but the costs of constructing the full-scale bridge prevented legislative action. When Paine asked Franklin what he should do, Franklin recommended he take the project to London or Paris, where he might secure the necessary funding to build it in England or France.

For some time, Paine had thought about traveling back to England to see his parents, now elderly. With peace achieved, his personal finances resolved, and hopes of securing endorsements and financing for his iron bridge, Paine departed for Europe on April 26, 1787. He intended to return the following winter, but events were to keep him away for 15 years.

In this piece of British propaganda against Paine's ideas, he stamps out ideals such as Morality, Justice, and National Prosperity, and endorses Treason, Misery, and Treachery.

CHAPTER

7

RIGHTS OF MAN

With his iron-bridge model stowed on board, Paine sailed to France. He had prophetically proclaimed America an example for the world, and its struggle the beginning of a world revolution. Yet, beyond the politicking required to secure official approval and funding of his project, the 50-year-old Paine had no intention of getting involved in European politics.

Paine had yet to grasp that his own role in the political dramas of the Age of Revolution was far from over. A revolution would also erupt in France, further energizing radical movements in England; and Paine himself would rise in defense of the former and make a fundamental contribution to the latter. The American radical was destined to become an international revolutionary.

In the 1780s, both Britain and France were experiencing revolutionary developments. Britain had lost the American colonies, but the growth of British capitalism and Britain's continued commercial supremacy provided the foundations for the first Industrial Revolution. Dramatic economic and social change would ensue, including a steady shift from family and household production to

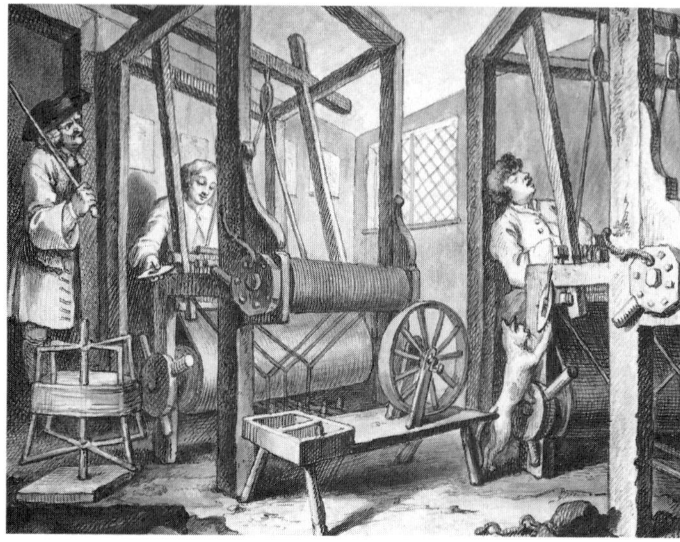

The master looks down on apprentices working at their looms. Workers saw the increased use of such machinery as oppressive and exploitative, and responded to it with acts of resistance and rebellion, including breaking machines.

factory work, the introduction of new techniques and technologies to the manufacturing process, an increase in urban populations (especially the working classes), and the growth of manufacturing towns and cities. Politically, middle- and working-class people continued to assert their rights as "free-born Englishmen," but they now began to insist that those rights included democracy, and they called for sweeping reform of the antiquated and corrupt English constitutional system.

Though ruled by a monarchy, France had supported the Americans against Britain. However, doing so had bankrupted the French government. Throughout the 18th century, France's rulers had sought to centralize the government, hoping to make it more efficient and less expensive. But the Old Regime of royal power and aristocratic privilege persisted, at great public expense. Those who had to cover the expenses of the king and the aristocracy through burdensome taxes were the French peasantry and the urban middle and working classes. Popular anger and resentment grew, and by the mid-1780s a crisis atmosphere prevailed. Under pressure from all sides, King Louis XVI called for a meeting in 1789 of the Estates-General, an assemblage of representatives from the three ranks of French society—the First Estate (aristocracy), the Second Estate (Catholic clergy), and the Third Estate (common people).

Paine arrived in France on May 26, 1787. He received a warm welcome, especially from the circle of elite figures—including the progressive-minded philosopher the Marquis de Condorcet—gathered around the Marquis de Lafayette. Uniting these men was a shared loyalty to the ideals of the 18th-century Enlightenment and a belief that humanity and society could be improved through the application of reason and the spread of freedom. Though an aristocrat, Lafayette himself, when only 20 years of age, had volunteered to serve the American cause and fought heroically as one of Washington's generals. Returning to France, he became renowned for his American military experience and his hopes of reforming French government and politics. Paine had first met him in Philadelphia, and they considered each other friends. In Paris, Paine also spent time in the company of a mutual friend, Thomas Jefferson, now American minister to France.

Paine presented his model bridge to France's most important intellectual and cultural institution, the French Academy, that summer. Although the academy granted its approval of his design, Paine's proposal to construct a bridge over the Seine was out of the question, given the government's financial straits. He had no choice but to take the project to England. In September—having been away for 13 years—he returned to England.

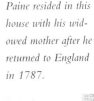

Paine resided in this house with his widowed mother after he returned to England in 1787.

After crossing the Channel, Paine quickly went up to Thetford to see his parents. He learned that his father had died the previous year. But his mother, now 90, was immensely pleased to see her son after so long, and she proudly told Tom how she fasted every July 4th in honor of his contributions to American independence. Before leaving for London, he arranged an allowance for her.

Paine also met Peter Whiteside, who had made a small fortune in America but had returned to Britain to promote American interests. Whiteside committed himself to Paine's plans and promised to help him apply for an English patent, which would grant Paine, as the original designer, exclusive rights to develop the projected bridge. Paine filed the necessary papers and journeyed back to Paris, returning again to London that summer. On August 26, 1788, his design was awarded a patent. He moved ahead with new confidence.

During the next 18 months, Paine traveled back and forth between Paris and London, forever seeking additional funds. He first planned to build a small, experimental version of his bridge (which may or may not have been completed) over the river Don, in the north of England near Sheffield. He would then create a larger (110-foot) model to be exhibited in northwest London in order to promote the grander scheme of erecting an iron bridge over the Thames. To carry out the work, Paine commissioned the Walker brothers of Rotherham. Unfortunately, though the London exhibition drew many visitors, it failed to attract new investors, and after a year, the Walkers had to dismantle it. Paine never did succeed in building his bridge; but his designs influenced more successful efforts, such as the iron bridge built in 1793 in northern England by Rowland Burdon over the Wear River at Sunderland.

Paine had devoted himself to the bridge project; however, even as he strove to accomplish it, he could not resist political engagement. In London, he met with reformers and radicals. And on his return visits to Paris, he joined Lafayette and Jefferson in discussing the deliberations taking place in the United States over the newly proposed Constitution. Moreover, from London he maintained a regular correspondence with Jefferson in which he reported on his meetings with British notables. He even briefly aspired to the post of U.S. minister to Britain, but to his disappointment, his old antagonist Gouverneur Morris received the appointment.

Nor did Paine limit himself to American questions. Within months of his arrival in Paris—at a time when Britain and France seemed on the verge of yet another war—Paine penned *Prospects on the Rubicon* (the title of which referred to Julius Caesar's crossing of Italy's Rubicon River in 49 B.C., fully committing him to war against Pompey). In this pamphlet, Paine argued for peace, contending that while there were those who would profit from war, it would hurt the majority, the working people and the poor, because they would have to bear the costs of war in heavier taxes.

The storming of the Bastille on July 14, 1789, was mainly a symbolic act, since the fortress was already scheduled for demolition. Oddly enough, Louis XVI made a one-word entry in his diary for that date: "Rien" *(meaning "nothing happened today").*

Still, what really drew Paine back into politics—even before the collapse of the bridge project—was the outbreak of the French Revolution in the summer of 1789. In June, the Third Estate reconstituted the Estates-General as the National Assembly, and soon after that as the Constituent Assembly, responsible for writing a constitution for the nation. On July 14—the recognized start of the Revolution—Parisian crowds stormed the Bastille, an ancient, disused prison that symbolized the oppressiveness of the Old Regime. Soon after, peasants rose up, attacking the landed estates of the aristocracy. Finally, the Constituent Assembly issued the so-called August decrees, abolishing feudalism and serfdom—the peasantry's hereditary obligations to work for, or pay cash dues, to aristocratic landlords. The assembly followed with the Declaration of the Rights of Man and of Citizens, establishing equality before the law, freedom of conscience and religion, and popular sovereignty, the principle that the government is constituted by the people.

In November, Lafayette, now commander of the National Guard, the new popular militia created by the revolutionary government, invited Paine back to France. With obvious pleasure Paine wrote to George Washington, "A share in two revolutions is living to some purpose." Though Lafayette and his closest allies in the assembly were not democrats (they had limited voting rights so as to exclude the majority of workingmen from elections), they had used their influence to push through a series of republican reforms, creating a constitutional monarchy and a more representative government. Impressed by these actions, Paine believed that the principles of the American Revolution were beginning to take hold, and imagining they could be realized with limited violence, he kept notes to write a book on the subject.

Paine pursued an active social calendar. In addition to frequent meetings with Jefferson and a reunion with Franklin, then in Paris, he made the acquaintance of diverse intellectuals, such as Adam Smith, the Scottish economist and author of *The Wealth of Nations* (1776), and the young Englishman Thomas Christie, who would later cofound the radical London Corresponding Society. Paine's friends introduced him to the Belgian baroness Cornélie de Vasse, who apparently desired a more intimate relationship than he was ready to offer.

In March 1790, Paine returned to London, bearing the key to the Bastille, which Lafayette had given him to pass on to Washington as a token of the French people's appreciation. Back in England, Paine found out that his mother had passed away. He also learned that the prominent Irish-born writer and member of Parliament, Edmund Burke, was preparing to write an attack on the French Revolution. This seriously agitated Paine. Early in the American Revolution, Burke had expressed sympathy for the American cause and had become a leader of the opposition in Parliament. Thus, on his return to England, Paine had contacted Burke and they had become friends, leading Paine to mistakenly assume that Burke, too, would be sympathetic to the changes in France. Unaware that he was arousing Burke's hostility, he had sent him a series of letters from Paris to keep him abreast of French developments.

Though Whig politician and writer Edmund Burke had defended the American colonists in their resistance to Britain, he vigorously opposed the French Revolution. He did not believe the common people capable of governing themselves.

Actually, while the radicalism of the French Revolution outraged Burke, what most worried him was its growing influence on British politics. He feared the spread of democratic and republican thinking and the possibility of a British revolution. He became convinced of this danger on reading a sermon delivered by the respected radical teacher and minister, Dr. Richard Price, in November 1789, on the anniversary of England's Glorious Revolution of 1688, which overthrew King James I in favor of the royal couple, William and Mary. Reinterpreting 1688 in the light of French events, Price asserted that the rights of Britons included the right to dispose of their governors when those governors threatened their rights.

Burke's *Reflections on the Revolution in France* appeared in November 1790. In it, he replied to the claims of Price and Paine, whom he referred to as the "new doctors of the rights of men," denounced the French revolutionaries, and praised the English constitution and political system. Yet Burke presented more than a defense of the existing political and social order. Burke authored the first great treatise of modern conservative political thought. Rejecting the spread of reason, revolution, innovation, and equality as dangerous, as leading inevitably to disaster, he firmly advocated tradition, preservation, continuity, and hierarchy.

Burke maintained that history tested institutions; therefore, if institutions such as monarchy and aristocracy had persisted, it meant they had stood the test of time and deserved respect and deference. Moreover, though change was possible and evident—on certain occasions even necessary and good—later generations were essentially bound to follow the precedents and compacts of their ancestors. By overthrowing historically tested institutions, Burke argued, revolutionaries invited not progress but chaos and tyranny. Referring to the common people as the "swinish multitude," Burke crassly revealed his disdain for popular politics and democracy.

The writings of Mary Wollstonecraft called for the recognition of the rights of women. She died after giving birth to her second child, Mary, who would marry the poet Percy Bysshe Shelley and write the novel Frankenstein.

Directed at the upper classes, Burke's *Reflections on the Revolution in France* became a literary success, selling 12,000 copies in a month and 20,000 in the first year, with French, Italian, and German translations appearing in rapid succession. At least 45 major replies were published, including *Letters to the Right Hon. Edmund Burke* by the radical Dissenter and scientist Joseph Priestley; *Vindiciae Gallicae: Defense of the French Revolution and Its English Admirers*, by the Scottish doctor and lawyer James Mackintosh; and *A Vindication of the Rights of Men* and *A Vindication of the Rights of Woman*, by the pioneering feminist Mary Wollstonecraft. But the most important—titled simply *Rights of Man*—came from Tom Paine. Indeed, the "debate" between Burke the conservative-elitist and Paine the radical-democrat established the very terms of modern political argument.

Begun as a single volume, *Rights of Man* would end up a two-part work. The first part, dedicated to George Washington, Paine wrote in London during the winter of 1790–91. First, he closely read Burke's pages. Then, with intense determination, he proceeded to defend the French Revolution and argue against hereditary power and privilege and for democracy and republican government. As he had done in *Common Sense*, Paine directed his words to people of all classes; but in particular, he intended them to inspire and activate working people, who still did not possess the right to vote. He hoped to rearticulate the popular understanding of the "rights of freeborn Englishmen" so as to encompass political equality and democracy.

Paine made sure to indicate where Burke's own sympathies lay. He referred to the rumor that the British government had hired Burke to write; he noted how Burke's own words showed that "[h]e is not affected by the reality of distress.... He pities the plumage [the deposed queen, Marie Antoinette] but forgets the dying bird [the oppressed French people]." Paine held that the "mob" actions that so upset Burke were a consequence and legacy of the violence and cruelties of aristocratic regimes.

To correct Burke's "selective" account of French events, Paine offered a more critical one. Including the *Declaration of the Rights of Man and of Citizens* in his own text, he emphasized how the French had rebelled not against the person of Louis XVI but against a "despotic" system and were now endeavoring to create a new one founded on republican principles. Against Burke's claims that each generation was obligated to defer to its ancestors, Paine insisted upon the "rights of the living" to determine their own lives, governments, and happiness. And to counter Burke's propositions about the historical origins of rights, Paine retorted that Burke did "not go far enough into antiquity." The rights of man, he wrote, went all the way back to "creation" and were in every generation "equal" and "universal" among men. Divinely ordained "natural rights" might be suppressed for periods of time, but they could not be forfeited or alienated.

Paine made a further distinction between natural rights and "civil rights," which grow out of them. Natural rights such as freedom of conscience and religion could be readily exercised by the individual; civil rights were those, such as security and protection, whose realization and enforcement depended upon a government created by people living in an organized society. In those terms, Paine considered the three sources of government: "superstition," the basis for priestly rule; "conquest," the basis for monarchy and aristocracy; and "reason," the basis for the authority of the people. In the last, free individuals "*entered into a compact with each other* to produce a government: and this is the only mode in which governments have a right to arise, and the only principle on which they have a right to exist."

Challenging Burke to display the English constitution (which he well knew was unwritten), Paine recounted that whereas in England government originated in the Norman Conquest of 1066, in France the Revolution had enabled the French people to reconstitute their government, basing it on reason and a popular compact. Observing that the French had established "universal right of conscience," Paine also urged the separation of church and state. Finally, he contended that whereas aristocratic states were warlike, republics were peace-loving.

Essentially declaring the British government illegitimate, Paine had some difficulty getting the work published. The originally commissioned publisher, Joseph Johnson, reneged after a visit by government agents. Paine next turned to another publisher, J. S. Jordan, located on Fleet Street, who consented to print it.

On March 13, 1791, *Rights of Man* was released. Its reception was as radical as its content. Within several weeks, 50,000 copies had been sold. Translations appeared. It made radicals ecstatic and the powerful anxious. Paine became one of Europe's best-known writers and, in Britain, the most controversial. The government considered taking action but hesitated for fear of generating further support for Paine.

Die
Rechte des Menschen.
Zweiter Theil.
Worin
Grundsatz und Ausübung
verbunden sind.
Von
Thomas Paine,
Sekretair der auswärtigen Angelegenheiten bei dem Congreß
während des Amerikanischen Krieges und Verfasser
des Werks, betitelt Common Sense.

Aus dem Englischen übersetzt.

THOMAS PAINE.

Zweyte Auflage.

Kopenhagen 1793.
Bey Christian Gottlob Proft, Sohn und Comp.

Rights of Man *appeared in translations everywhere; this is the title page of a German-language edition published in 1793. Paine's arguments inspired radicals and worried the powerful around the world.*

In April, Paine went back to Paris for three months, again hosted by Lafayette. There he commenced work on a sequel to *Rights of Man*, and this would eventually become Part II of the book. Anticipating great things in both France and Britain, and persistently optimistic that serious bloodshed could be avoided, Paine ignored the dangers emerging on both sides of the Channel, such as the increasing violence in the streets of Paris (which, on at least one occasion, threatened his own life).

On the morning of June 21, Lafayette woke Paine to tell him that Louis XVI and the royal family had escaped from Paris and were on their way to join the conservative forces mobilizing under Austrian command. Paine hoped they would not be caught, believing it would prevent vengeful violence. But they were captured at Varennes and returned to the capital. The incident ignited popular anger and furthered the divisions growing among the more moderate and more radical revolutionary groups. Distancing himself from Lafayette, who still wanted a constitutional monarchy, Paine helped Condorcet found the Republican Society and a short-lived journal, the *Republican.* Paine himself drafted the society's manifesto, calling for an end to the monarchy. On July 1, he and his comrades nailed their manifesto to the door of the building where the Constituent Assembly met. It created a tremendous furor.

Persuaded that republicanism would triumph in France, Paine returned to London on July 13. He stayed at the home of Clio Rickman, a close friend from his Lewes days, and continued to work on Part II of *Rights of Man.* He also met with other prominent radicals, including the scientist Joseph Priestley, the feminist Mary Wollstonecraft, the philosopher William Godwin, and the political writer John Horne Tooke.

Under the influence of the events in France, England experienced the growth of new political movements, both radical and conservative. Organized in January 1792 by the shoemaker Thomas Hardy, the London Corresponding Society, composed in the majority of "tradesmen, mechanics and shopkeepers," established a radical, pro-democracy network that included similar groups around Britain. Faced with the spread of pro-French, republican sentiments, British officials initiated several countermeasures. They assigned spies to track radicals' activities and encouraged conservative "Church and King" mobs—so named for their shouts in support of the Church of England and the English monarchy—to attack the homes of radical figures, including Priestley's Birmingham residence and laboratories. The assaults compelled him to move to London and, eventually, to the United States.

The British government targeted Paine in particular. Among other things, Paine's enemies hired the ardent royalist George Chalmers, a civil servant, to produce a scurrilous biography of him, which Chalmers wrote under the pseudonym Francis Oldys. Paine resisted the temptation of responding. Rather, he occupied himself with his own book and made occasional appearances at radical gatherings, always receiving an enthusiastic response.

When Paine finished Part II of *Rights of Man*, he dedicated the book to Lafayette. As before, he had difficulty getting the new work into print; however, once again he was able to turn to J. S. Jordan. It was published on February 16, 1792, and its reception exceeded even that of Part I. The work brimmed with optimism. "I do not believe that monarchy and aristocracy will continue seven years longer in any of the enlightened countries of Europe," Paine wrote, and he blatantly called for a British revolution (though peaceful). Paine opened the book with paeans to the United States: "What Archimedes said of the mechanical powers, may be applied to Reason and Liberty: 'Had we,' said he, 'a place to stand upon, we might raise the world.' The revolution of America presented in politics what was only theory in mechanics." Paragraphs later, he pronounced: "If universal peace, civilization, and commerce, are ever to be the happy lot of man, it cannot be accomplished but by a revolution in the system of government." And, before finishing, he confessed to being an international revolutionary: "[M]y country is the world, and my religion is to do good."

Paine restated his previous arguments regarding the despotism and backwardness of kingly and aristocratic government and the justice and progressive possibilities of democratic republicanism. Now he added the question of class inequality to his case: Monarchy and aristocracy necessarily entailed "excess and inequality of taxation," throwing the "great mass of the community...into poverty and discontent." Describing the British and other European governments as feeding off the blood of the populace, Paine wondered at their pride: "When, in countries that are called civilized, we see age going to the workhouse and youth to the gallows, something must be wrong in the system of government.... Why is it, that scarcely any are executed but the poor?" And yet, he wrote, as the United States demonstrated, it need not be this way: "There the poor are not oppressed, the rich are not privileged."

While lauding the United States, Paine had nothing good to say about British government and its illusionary constitution: "From want of a constitution in England to restrain the wild impulse of power, many of the laws are irrational and tyrannical.... Government by precedent, without any regard to the principle of precedent, is one of the vilest systems that can be set up."

Turning to the subject of social classes, Paine suggested an estate tax to limit the amount of property that could be accumulated by inheritance. He also recommended a series of social programs designed to create economic democracy. Specifically, he proposed that government provide income to the poor and special relief to families with children; pensions for the elderly; public funding of education; financial support for newly married couples and new mothers; funeral expenses for the working poor; and job centers to address unemployment. Outlining how all this could be accomplished, Paine insisted that, with a radical change in government, taxation could actually be reduced. A nation following this plan, he wrote, could then glory in its accomplishments:

> When it shall be said in any country in the world, my poor are happy; neither ignorance nor distress is to be found among them; my jails are empty of prisoners, my streets of beggars; the aged are not in want, the taxes are

> not oppressive; the rational world is my friend, because I am the friend of its happiness: when these things can be said, then may that country boast its constitution and its government.

Calling for a reduction in naval warships and the formation of an Anglo-French-Dutch peace alliance, and envisioning the independence of the Latin American people, Paine predicted that the present age would be known as the "Age of Reason." Finally, returning once more to the matter that had disturbed his childhood, he stated that "*every religion is good, that teaches man to be good.*"

Paine brilliantly crafted his words and arguments so as to engage the aspirations and imaginations of the common people, especially to the artisan class from which he himself had emerged. Their appeal reached well beyond Britain. Translations appeared again in French, Dutch, and German. In Ireland, popular musicians honored Paine and his work with a hornpipe melody, "The Rights of Man." Estimated to have sold almost 500,000 copies in the course of the next 10 years, the complete *Rights of Man* became the best-selling book ever published in English.

The publication of the second part of *Rights of Man* led the British government to intensify its antiradical campaigns. Paine's supporters rallied, but so did the opposition. Royalist mobs even took to burning effigies of Paine; concerned about his safety, his friends persuaded him to retreat to Bromley, a village south of London. He remained away only a short time. On May 21, 1792, the government, hoping to suppress Paine's work, issued a proclamation "against wicked and seditious writings" and summoned Paine to appear in court in June. However, when the day arrived, the government requested a six-month postponement.

Paine defiantly continued to write. He also sat for a portrait by the painter George Romney. Ironically, while the British government escalated its repression of Paine and other radicals, in August the French government honored

In response to the popular success of Rights of Man, *several publications appeared attacking Paine's character and ideas. In this illustration to one such work, Paine hangs by his own words.*

Paine and a small number of other foreigners for having "served the cause of liberty and prepared the emancipation of the people" by making them French citizens. Soon after that, the city of Calais elected him a delegate to the National Convention, which was set to meet that September to write a new French constitution.

Nevertheless, by summer's end, the continued attacks and repression began to take their toll on Paine's spirit. His friends worried about what might happen next. It is said that on September 13, the poet William Blake, hearing that a warrant had been issued for Paine's arrest, warned him: "You must not go home, or you are a dead man!"

Heeding this advice, Paine decided to leave for France that very evening. Accompanied by John Frost, the lawyer for the London Corresponding Society, and Achille Audibert, a Calais official, he traveled through the night to the port of Dover. There the three checked into the York Hotel, planning to embark in the morning. However, local officials were apparently prepared for Paine's attempt at departure. They demanded to inspect his belongings. After heated exchanges, persistent harassment, and the confiscation of selected documents, they allowed him to repack his belongings and board the ship with Frost and Audibert. At the dock, a royalist crowd had gathered (or been organized!) to jeer, taunt, and threaten. Rattled, Paine took refuge below deck. On September 14, he sailed from Dover, never again to return to England.

The government had succeeded in driving Paine out of Britain. Not yet fully satisfied, the government put him on trial (in absentia) in December, charging him with "seditious libel." His attorney defended him in the name of "liberty of the press." A hand-picked jury returned a guilty verdict. The streets filled with Paine's supporters, but the verdict stood. By the use of such measures, the government eventually suppressed the radical movement.

A democratic-republican revolution would never come to pass in Britain, but after going underground for a generation, radicalism and the working-class struggle for democracy would reemerge and commence a slow but steady transformation of the British polity. And Paine's *Rights of Man* would be appreciated as a foundation text of the movement.

On August 10, 1792, Parisian artisans marched on the Tuileries Palace to demand an end to the monarchy. Fired on by defenders, the crowd attacked and killed 500 of the king's Swiss Guard. The king and queen fled to the National Assembly.

CHAPTER

8

TRIALS AND TRIBULATIONS

Paine disembarked at the port of Calais not as a refugee escaping British authorities but as a French citizen. And the people of Calais, who had elected him to represent them in the new National Convention, afforded him a glorious reception. His companion John Frost recorded:

> All the soldiers on duty were drawn up; the officer of the guard embraced [Paine] on landing, and presented him with the national cockade, which a handsome young woman, who was standing by, begged the honor of fixing it in his hat, and returned it to him, expressing a hope that he would continue his exertions in the behalf of Liberty, France, and the Rights of Man. A salute was then fired from the battery to announce to the people of Calais the arrival of their new representative.

After the abuse and ridicule Paine had suffered in Dover, Calais's welcome must have greatly lifted his spirits. All the way to Paris the French celebrated him, leading Frost to observe, "I believe he is rather fatigued with the kissing."

Unfortunately, the adulation Paine received and the apparent unity and joy he experienced gave him no warning of what he was soon to face. He had followed French developments, but he was not necessarily prepared. The same events that had led to his honors had engendered dangerous new political divisions capable of destroying the Revolution and all those associated with it.

In September 1791, the Constituent Assembly had adopted a constitution that outraged republicans and antagonized urban workers, the *sans-culottes* (literally, those without culottes, the knee-length breeches worn by upper-class men; workingmen wore full-length pants). Although the new constitution provided for the election of a new National Assembly and drastically reformed government and political life, it established a constitutional monarchy, not a republic. The king remained head of state. Furthermore, splitting Frenchmen into "active" and "passive" citizens based on property ownership, it granted only those with property the right to vote. But, enfranchised or not, the sans-culottes would not remain passive.

Proponents of constitutional monarchy dominated the newly elected National Assembly. Republicans were also well represented, but they had soon divided into moderate and radical factions, the former coming to be known as Girondins (because their leaders were from the Gironde region in southwestern France) and the latter as Jacobins (after their regular meeting place, the Parisian monastery of the Dominican friars, who are called Jacobins in France). Led by the journalist Jacques-Pierre Brissot de Warville, the Girondins favored private property and the free market, believed in calm and reasoned deliberation, and drew their support from the more prosperous citizenry. The more ruthless Jacobins, led by the lawyer Maximilien Robespierre, favored democracy, believed in deliberate and swift action, and drew their support from the sans-culottes. In the assembly, the two factions difffered immediately over the question of war.

In August 1791, Austria and Prussia had threatened military intervention to reestablish the French monarchy's authority. The new constitution pacified them, but the threat remained, instigating strange alliances within French politics. The Girondins proposed the pursuit of a preemptive revolutionary crusade against Europe's absolute monarchies. The Jacobins—for the time being, at least—opposed the idea. They knew that France's army was ill prepared, and they were convinced that the lower classes, as ever, would suffer the consequences. However, King Louis XVI and his sympathizers supported the Girondins, hoping that France's likely defeat would lead to a restoration of the Old Regime. In April 1792, France went to war against Austria and Prussia.

By summer the war was going badly for France. Convinced that the revolution was imperiled, not only by foreign enemies but also by French royalists and moderates, the sans-culottes took to the streets in militant demonstrations. Never close to the lower classes, the Girondins could neither calm their anxieties nor constrain their actions. In early August the sans-culottes demanded King Louis's abdication, and Robespierre called for a new National Convention and a more democratic constitution. Finally, on August 10, the Parisian sans-culottes, with Jacobin encouragement, mounted a violent insurrection, effectively deposing the king.

With Louis and his family locked away in a medieval fortress, the National Assembly scheduled elections for a National Convention. Yet violence continued. Austrian and Prussian troops moved into France, generating fresh fears and rumors of conspiracy and counterrevolution. In early September mobs stormed the country's prisons and massacred more than 1,000 inmates, believing them potential allies of the foreign invaders.

Not having witnessed the violence and horrors of the situation, Paine returned to France with hope and optimism, eager to involve himself directly in France's revolutionary politics. Arriving in the capital on September 19, he took rooms at White's Hotel. Other American, British, and Irish radicals also came to reside there, providing Paine with a circle of English-speaking companions. He and his comrades soon organized a club, Friends of the Rights of Man, leading the owners to rename the place the Hotel Philadelphia. Members dined and drank together, shared news from home, argued politics and ideas, and discussed prospects and plans for revolutionary risings in Britain and Ireland.

The morning after his arrival, Paine paid a visit to the U.S. minister to France, his old political enemy Gouverneur Morris (who still had no affection for Paine). He then attended the opening of the National Convention at the great hall adjacent to the old Tuileries palace. In the next few days—excited by news of the French army's first victory over the Austrian-Prussian forces, at Valmy in northeastern France—the 750 delegates enthusiastically abolished royalty and declared that "the French Republic is one and indivisible."

Paine may have thought it would be otherwise, but his participation in the convention promised to be difficult. With limited French, he would have to depend on others to translate the deliberations and, in turn, his own remarks. He still tended to see things in terms of his experiences in the American Revolution. And having been away from Paris, he was unfamiliar with the latest intricacies and divisions of French politics. Paine's friend and original guide, the Marquis de Lafayette, was gone, having disgraced himself by ordering his troops to fire on a demonstration of sans-culottes. Reassigned to the battlefield, he defected to the Austrians, who imprisoned him for the duration of the war.

Convention delegates fell into three groups: the Girondins; the Jacobins, also called the Mountain because they sat in elevated seats on the left side of the hall; and the unaffiliated majority, known as the Plain, because they sat on the low seats between the two parties, which competed for their votes. Initially, the Girondins well outnumbered their Jacobin opponents, giving them leadership of the government. However, the latter were prepared to exploit every opportunity.

In early exchanges, Paine quickly exhibited his innocence and ignorance of convention politics. Realizing his errors, he did not rush to take sides but instead tried to inspire solidarity. In his *Letter to the People of France,* published in late September by his friend the journalist and editor Nicolas de Bonneville, Paine praised France's leadership of Europe's revolution for "liberty and equality" and called for unity in the campaigns ahead. His words were ignored.

At the end of September the convention appointed nine of its members, including Paine, to draft a new constitution. Paine wrote the accompanying Declaration of Rights. The Marquis de Condorcet, another old friend, led the committee and wrote most of the main text. The finished product ended up reading more like a dissertation than a constitution. Condorcet spent too long drafting it and produced an overly long and detailed document. Presented in early 1793, it was rejected by Girondins and Jacobins alike.

Given Paine's artisan upbringing and democratic commitments, it might have been expected he would ally himself with the Jacobins. However, he came to be identified with the Girondins. It was not simply the case, however, that Paine's views had moderated with age (he was now 55). It was more a case of personal loyalty and intellectual affinity. Brissot de Warville and the other Girondins leaders—almost all of whom were fluent in English and revered the American Revolution—had befriended Paine during his previous stays in France. More than that, Paine shared the Girondins' pronounced aspiration to spread republican revolution beyond France's borders; he subscribed to their belief in private property and free markets; and he ultimately agreed with them on the critical matter of what was to be done with Louis XVI, now more often referred to as Louis Capet. Louis-Antoine de Saint-Just, a young lawyer and devoted follower of Robespierre, had argued for executing the king without a trial. Others replied that with the monarchy abolished, there was no need to take further action on the matter. Most delegates stood somewhere in the middle. However, the discovery of secret papers revealed that the king had corresponded and conspired with France's enemies, which strengthened the case for a speedy execution.

Paine sought to put off the worst, hoping to find an alternative. He had championed the struggle against monarchy. He was ready to see Louis tried and punished, but—abhorring capital punishment—he opposed sentencing the deposed king to death. Furthermore, knowing Americans had not forgotten that Louis's government had aided them against the British, he worried that an execution would antagonize the United States just when the French most needed U.S. support. Paine pressed for a trial, saying that hearings might serve to expose the extent of the conspiracy and further demonstrate the "necessity of revolutions" against monarchy.

The trial opened in late December (strangely coinciding with Paine's own trial in London). Louis was brought before the convention. Though he did not challenge its authority, he refused to acknowledge guilt. The Jacobins called for a quick verdict and a quick execution. The Girondins suggested a national plebiscite. Paine wanted to keep the decision in the hands of the convention, but he campaigned vigorously against a death sentence. Addressing the delegates, he proposed that they set an example for the world by abolishing the death penalty altogether and exiling the king and his family to the United States. "it is our duty as Legislators," he said, "not to spill a drop of blood, when our purpose may be effectually accomplished without it." Recalled and praising Robespierre's own earlier call to abolish the death penalty, Paine continued,

> Monarchical Governments have trained the human race, and inured it to the sanguinary arts and refinements of punishment; and it is exactly the same punishment, which has so long shocked the sight, and tormented the patience of the People, that now, in their turn, they practise in revenge on their oppressors. But it becomes us to be strictly on our guard against the abomination and perversity of Monarchical examples; as France has been the first of European Nations to abolish Royalty, let her also be the first to abolish the Punishment of Death, and to find out a milder and more effectual substitute.

In his trial before the National Convention, King Louis XVI refused to acknowledge guilt for the charges brought against him. But his guilt was never in doubt; the real question under debate was whether he should suffer the death penalty.

Paine persuaded many, but not enough. In mid-January 1793, he joined a near-unanimous convention in finding Louis guilty. Then, against Paine's hopes and efforts, the delegates voted, by the slimmest of margins, to sentence Louis to death. Again Paine spoke up, trying to prevent the sentence from being carried out. He faced fierce opposition and repeated interruptions, especially from the Jacobin Jean-Paul Marat, a doctor-turned-journalist who possessed a tremendous following among the sans-culottes. The convention reaffirmed its decision, and on January 21, Louis was taken to the guillotine and beheaded.

Although Paine had not sided with the Girondins on every question, his opposition to the king's execution incensed the Mountain. He maintained friendly ties with certain prominent Jacobins, most notably the lawyer Georges Danton, but he had made enemies of most of the others. In time, they would act against him.

The trial and execution of the king strengthened the Jacobins, and in the ensuing months their power, influence, and popular support grew. The Girondins could not control events. In February, France declared war against Britain and Holland, and those countries joined with Austria, Prussia, Russia, and Spain in an alliance aimed at nullifying the French Revolution. Faced with this array of opponents, France's army suffered a series of defeats. In response to a new military draft, peasants in the Vendée, a western region

On January 21, 1793, Louis XVI was executed by guillotine. Compared to other methods, the guillotine was a swift and humane mode of execution. Its namesake, Dr. Joseph Guillotin, had campaigned to extend its use to the execution of individuals from all social classes, not just the aristocracy.

of France, rose up in rebellion. Economic conditions deteriorated throughout the country, and food shortages occurred. In Paris, there were angry calls for price controls. The Girondins resisted. The Jacobins, eager to further attract the sans-culottes to their cause, adopted the demands as their own.

Growing desperate, the Girondins responded with attacks against leading Jacobins. They went after Danton, who ably turned back their criticisms and even secured the creation of a Committee of Public Safety with himself a leading member. Next the Girondins attempted to prosecute Marat, now president of the Jacobin Club, who had taken to issuing fiery and threatening broadsides. In April the Girondins ordered him to be tried for inciting riots and seeking to destroy the National Convention.

After Louis's execution, Paine had thought about returning to the United States, but he feared he would be caught at sea by the British. Remaining in France, he essentially withdrew from the convention and moved out to a small house in Saint-Denis, some ten miles from the center of Paris. There he rested and entertained a string of diverse visitors such as Clio Rickman, his old and dear friend from Lewes and London, now residing in France; Mary Wollstonecraft, the English feminist; and Brissot de Warville, the Girondin leader. However, Marat's trial brought Paine back into Paris and the political fray. Paine—despising Marat as much as Marat despised him—testified against the Jacobin regarding the attempted suicide of Paine's fellow Englishman and Saint-Denis boarder, William Johnson. Johnson claimed his act had been inspired by Marat's calls for revolutionary violence, for he believed Marat had targeted foreigners for death, and he preferred to die by his own hand.

Marat was acquitted of all charges; the verdict depressed Paine but thrilled the sans-culottes. Jacobin power swelled. Given the persistently bad news from the battlefront and events in Paris, Paine now began to lose all hope in the Revolution. He expressed his concerns in a letter to Danton and, in correspondence with Thomas Jefferson, who shared Paine's revolutionary sympathies, he admitted his despair and spoke again of "returning home."

Tensions continued to mount. Feeling themselves under siege in the capital, the Girondins sought provincial support, further agitating the Jacobins and their Parisian allies among the sans-culottes. Confrontations ensued in late May as the sans-culottes organized for another insurrection. Then, on June 2, demonstrators surrounded the Tuileries and demanded the arrest of the Girondin leadership. Paine rushed to the palace. There he encountered Danton, who, expressing concern for Paine's safety, warned him not to enter the palace, for it might lead to his name being added to the arrest list. Paine sadly remarked that the Revolution, like the Roman god Saturn, had started to "devour its own children." Danton answered, "Revolutions cannot be made with rosewater." The convention acceded to the crowd's demands. The Jacobins had broken the Girondins. Soon the Mountain became the leading force in the convention.

Throughout the summer, conditions deteriorated still further. The French army retreated. Provincial uprisings spread. Food riots continued in the capital. A young Girondin, Charlotte Corday, assassinated Marat. All of these events enabled the Jacobins to tighten their grip on power. In June they produced a liberal and democratic constitution but almost immediately suspended it. In July the Jacobins reconstituted the Committee of Public Safety as the National Convention's executive authority, removing the increasingly moderate Danton and appointing the radicals Robespierre and Saint-Just to membership. They also took control of the Revolutionary Tribunal, which was responsible for trying "enemies of the Revolution." By autumn the nation would be subject to Jacobin dictatorship and the infamous Reign of Terror.

The Jacobin-led government did accomplish things. In late August it ordered a total mobilization of the citizenry in defense of the Revolution, thereby enabling it to recruit fresh military battalions and set up workshops to supply them. With a million men under arms, France's army suppressed the provincial risings and began to turn the tide of war at the front. Moreover, the Jacobins stabilized the economy by fixing prices and wages. Foodstuffs returned to the markets.

Nevertheless, the same Jacobin regime—propelled both by its own ambitions and by the anxious demands of the sans-culottes—also commenced a brutal campaign to eliminate "enemies" at home. In October the Revolutionary Tribunal prosecuted the Girondin leaders, Brissot de Warville included, and then ordered their execution at the guillotine. The Terror had begun.

In the wake of the June events, Paine had withdrawn again to Saint-Denis. Depressed about the direction of the revolution and worried about his personal safety, he drank heavily. Of course, he had good reason to worry. Certain Jacobins had taken to passing outrageous rumors that he too had engaged in conspiracies against the government. In September—possibly hoping to redeem himself, possibly hoping to distract them from the secret plans he was concocting to leave for the United States—Paine offered to serve the Jacobins as an adviser on American affairs. But neither his efforts with the Jacobins nor his plans to escape France proved successful.

Amid the prosecutions and deaths of his Girondin friends, and continuing purges, trials, and executions, Paine's own arrest seemed inevitable. Yet he did not sit idly waiting. He had long planned to write something on the subject of religion. He now dedicated himself to that project, not only because he faced mortal dangers but also in response to a Jacobin offensive against the Catholic Church and Christian beliefs.

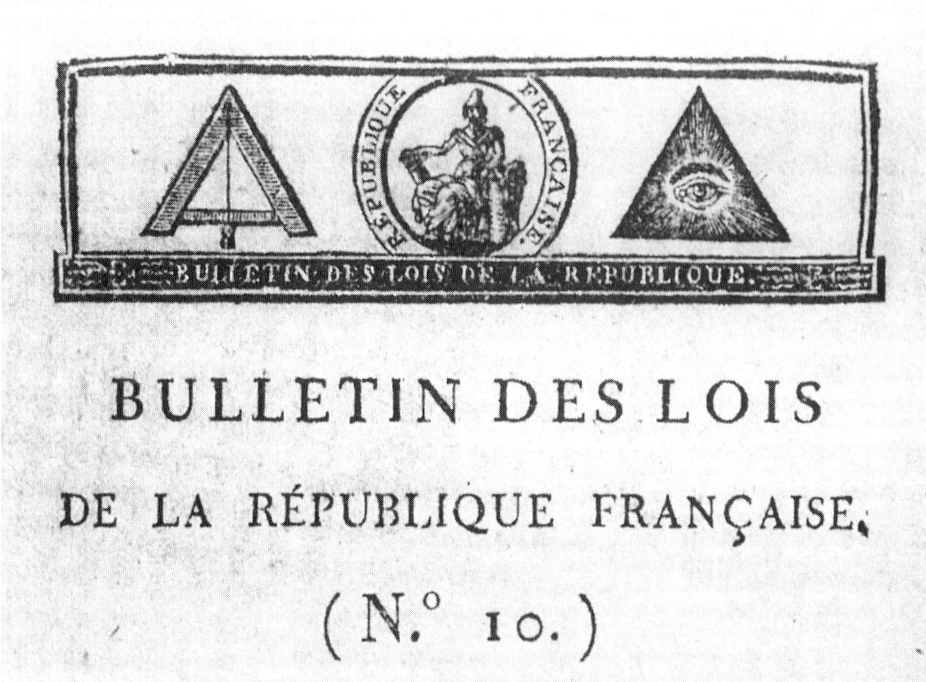

The heading of the Bulletin des lois, *a bulletin published to disseminate laws throughout the French Republic, contains three symbols of the ideals important to the new regime. The goddess of Liberty is flanked by a carpenter's level, representing equality, and an all-seeing eye, representing God.*

The anti-Christian campaigns did not originate with the Jacobins. In 1789, the Constituent Assembly had confiscated church lands, and in 1790, it had subordinated the clergy to government authority. In the three years since, revolutionaries had subjected the Church and the clergy to continual persecution and attack. However, in the autumn of 1793, the Jacobin-led convention made "dechristianization" official state policy. Wiping out all references to the "Christian era" by replacing the saint's days with republican feast days, the convention issued a completely new calendar that was backdated to the foundation of the Republic in 1792 ("Year One of the Revolution"). It renamed Notre Dame cathedral the Temple of Reason and posted a sign outside the building declaring, "Death is an eternal sleep." Eventually, the government was to close all the churches of Paris.

It was against this background that Paine wrote *The Age of Reason*. He wrote it in two stages (and originally published it in two parts) and dedicated it "To My Fellow Citizens of the United States of America." Ironically enough, it has forever remained his most controversial book, especially in the United States.

In *The Age of Reason*, Paine mounted a direct assault on organized religion. He blunty asserted, "All national institutions of churches, whether Jewish, Christian or Turkish, appear to me no other than human inventions, set up to terrify and enslave mankind, and monopolize power and profit." Intent upon revealing the contents of the Bible to be no more than a grand mythology imposed on humanity by priests and clerics for "purposes of power and revenue," he proceeded to render a critical examination of the Old and New Testaments from Adam and Eve to Jesus Christ.

Paine's perennial critics have regularly misrepresented *The Age of Reason* as the work of a nonbeliever. But Paine was no atheist. Indeed, he wrote *The Age of Reason* as a profession of faith and a reaction to the atheism he believed motivated the dechristianization movement in France. At the very outset he stated, "I believe in one God, and no more; and I hope for happiness beyond this life." He added, "I believe in the equality of man; and I believe that religious duties consist in doing justice, loving mercy, and endeavoring to make our fellow-creatures happy. I do not believe... in the creed of any church I know of. My own mind is my own church."

Raised by an Anglican mother and a Quaker father, and having preached as a Methodist, Paine in his maturity had arrived at deism, a belief in God as Creator, the first cause of the universe. Against those who would say his arguments denied "revelation," Paine maintained that the true revelation was the Creation itself: "THE WORD OF GOD IS THE CREATION WE BEHOLD and it is in this word, which no human invention can counterfeit or alter, that God speaketh universally to man." The path to understanding God's revelation lay through reasoned reflection and natural philosophy (the sciences). Finally, Paine believed that the magnificence and bountifulness of the Creation attested to God's generosity and obliged humans to serve God by "imitating" his generosity and moral goodness.

Though Paine may have welcomed the revolutionary downsizing of the Catholic Church, as an ardent believer in separating church and state and guaranteeing freedom of religion, he definitely opposed both the original revolutionary policy of making religion an arm of the state and the new one of making religion an enemy of the state. It also concerned him that dechristianization might entail the loss of religion's better values, "of morality, of humanity, and of the theology that is true."

Deism did not originate with Paine, nor did he stand alone in his beliefs. It had roots in the 17th century, and Paine's contemporary fellow deists included his American friends Thomas Jefferson and Benjamin Franklin and his French antagonist Robespierre. (Though Robespierre, like Paine, perceived much of the dechristianization drive to be inspired by atheism, in May 1794 he did something Paine would not have done. He persuaded the National Convention to establish the "Cult of the Supreme Being" as the nation's official religion.)

Paine's great mischief in *The Age of Reason*—as ever—was to make understandable and accessible to the laboring classes ideas that had previously circulated only among the higher social ranks. Just like his previous revolutionary pamphlets, *The Age of Reason* became a bestseller, both inspiring and upsetting wide readerships on both sides of the Atlantic. And once again, Paine provided a foundation text of modern culture. *The Age of Reason* soon came to serve as a manifesto—a kind of bible in its own right—for other deists, freethinkers, and critics of religious authority and dogma. But its very success and influence would later haunt

Paine upon his return to the United States, where many religious folk had come to see him as an agent of the devil for his blasphemy.

In late November 1793, Robespierre called upon the Revolutionary Tribunal to attend to "foreign conspirators" dwelling in France. Aware of what that meant, Paine hurried to finish his work, completing what would appear as Part I on Christmas Eve. That evening he went into Paris to celebrate with friends at White's Hotel and stayed for the night. At four in the morning he was awakened by the police and taken into custody. He persuaded them to take him to his house in Saint-Denis before escorting him to prison, and there he was able to hand over the manuscript for *The Age of Reason* to a friend, the American radical and writer Joel Barlow. That afternoon Paine was taken to the Luxembourg Palace, which had been converted to a prison as the numbers incarcerated continued to increase. American friends in Paris immediately tried to gain Paine's release, but they failed. Paine himself desperately sought the aid of Gouverneur Morris, who failed to take action, for reasons either diplomatic or personal, or both.

At first, the daily regimen at the Luxembourg was not so terrible. Following morning chores, prisoners were permitted to mingle, and Paine regularly met with other inmates to discuss the latest developments. He received correspondence and newspapers; by candlelight, he read and continued to make notes on religion. But as the Jacobins escalated the Terror in the spring of 1794, they imposed tighter controls on the prisons, effectively cutting off Paine and his fellow inmates from the outside world.

At the end of March, the Terror seized Danton. Arriving at the Luxembourg, he remarked to Paine, "That which you did for the happiness and liberty of your country, I tried in vain to do for mine.... They will send me to the scaffold.... I shall go gaily." A couple of weeks later Danton was executed. The shadow of the guillotine hung over all the prisoners. Paine fought despondency. He wrote poetry, worked on Part II of *The Age of Reason* and continued to meet prison colleagues to talk about politics and religion.

In June, the Terror intensified still further, and executions accelerated. Simply being "denounced" served as warrant for arrest and execution. Before it was halted, the Terror accounted for almost 18,000 executions. Including those who died in prison, the victims totaled more than 35,000.

After six months' confinement, Paine collapsed with a fever that would last two weeks. His three Belgian cellmates ministered to him, fighting to save him though they believed he would die. Paine not only survived the fever; a miraculous mistake saved him from the guillotine.

On July 24, the public prosecutor scheduled Paine for execution. The next morning, as was the practice, prison officers passed through the Luxembourg's corridors to make a chalk mark on the doors of those due to be collected later on for execution. It happened that on the previous evening, Paine's Belgian comrades had asked permission to keep their cell door open, so that a breeze might enter and cool their feverish patient. The door was still open in the morning, and when the officers entered the cell, they mistakenly placed their chalk mark on the wrong side. Thus the mark could not be seen from the corridor when the door was closed, and when the guards later came to collect the next day's victims, they passed right by Paine's cell.

On July 27, before the authorities could rectify the error, Robespierre fell from power. The sans-culottes, estranged by recent Jacobin actions, did not intervene to save their former hero. The following day, Robespierre died at the guillotine, and the Terror ceased. Men from the political faction previously known as the Plain—they were now called Thermidorians, after the month of the revolutionary calendar in which they took power—replaced those of the Mountain.

Barely recovered from his illness, Paine wrote to the National Convention seeking release. Though the Thermidorians relaxed prison regulations, they did not agree to his request. In August, however, his prospects changed dramatically when the U.S. government replaced Morris as its representative with James Monroe, a former U.S. Senator from Virginia who agreed with Paine and supported the French Revolution. (Monroe was destined to become secretary of state under President James Madison and, in 1817, the fifth President of the United States.)

Monroe acknowledged Paine as a U.S. citizen and worked to secure his release. After a series of disappointments, Paine finally left the Luxembourg on November 5. He had spent 10 months in prison. But he was now free.

Born in Corsica, Napoleon Bonaparte began his career as a lieutenant of artillery. His military successes made him a national hero in France, and his military and political genius enabled him to secure power and establish himself as virtual dictator of the country in 1799.

CHAPTER

9

MATTERS OF JUSTICE

Twenty years Paine's junior, the new U.S. minister to France, James Monroe, had the greatest respect and admiration for the 57-year-old radical. Having secured his release from the Luxembourg, Monroe took Paine to his own residence, inviting him to remain with him and Mrs. Monroe, at least until he recovered from his imprisonment. Paine had developed a large abscess in his side, which terribly discomforted him and occasionally made him ill. He was soon able to get out and about, yet he would remain a guest of the Monroes for almost two years. He spoke of returning to the United States, but he would not finally do so until 1802. In the meantime, he again involved himself in French political affairs, which, though never again as violent or horrific as during the Terror, remained dangerous and turbulent.

The French Revolution did not come to a halt with Robespierre's demise; however, neither the revolutionary aspirations of the Girondins or Jacobins, nor the movements of the sans-culottes, ever regained the momentum or influence they had in the early 1790s. All the more, France became a country in which the rich grew richer and the poor grew poorer. The Thermidorians eliminated the radical presence in government, terminated the economic controls instituted by the Jacobins, and prepared a new constitution that ultimately limited democracy by restoring voting-rights distinctions based on property and wealth. The suppression of Catholicism continued. In 1795, the Thermidorians installed a new government structure consisting of a two-chamber legislature headed by a five-man executive called the Directory.

The Directory did not go unopposed. In the spring of 1797, it was compelled to suppress the radical "Conspiracy of Equals" and arrest its organizer, François-Noel "Gracchus" Babeuf, a journalist of humble background. Proclaiming that "Nature has given to every man the right

John Jay served as the first chief justice of the United States. During his Supreme Court term he negotiated the very unpopular Jay Treaty, establishing closer commercial relations between Britain and the United States. Protesters burned him in effigy.

to the enjoyment of an equal share in property," Babeuf had espoused a vision of agrarian communism and begun to recruit sans-culottes and peasants to his cause. He was executed on May 27. Moreover, a resurgence of royalist sympathy that same year posed a far greater threat to the new government than had Babeuf's movement. In September the Directory arranged for the arrest of the pro-royalist leadership; by either deporting or executing these and other opponents, the Directory exercised dictatorial rule.

Government by the Directory lasted until 1799, when a military coup established a three-man "Consular" regime that included the ambitious Napoleon Bonaparte, the greatest of French generals. France had remained at war with the monarchies of Europe throughout these years, and Napoleon's fame and public stature had dramatically risen (and sometimes fallen) with his military campaigns. The Consulate simply paved the way for Napoleon's personal rule and imperial ambitions. It also brought the French Revolution to an end.

Just weeks after Paine's release in November 1794, he was reinstated to the National Convention. As much as he appreciated aspects of the constitution proposed by the Thermidorians, Paine found it impossible to tolerate their attempts to reverse the democratic political advances embodied in the suspended Constitution of 1793. Specifically, he could not abide dividing the citizenry along the lines of wealth. Early in the summer of 1795, he wrote *Dissertation on First Principles of Government,* publicly reaffirming his commitment to democracy, republican government, and equal civil and political rights. On July 7, he reiterated those points in a speech to the convention. But his arguments made little difference. The Thermidorians followed through with their plans.

Paine withdrew from the soon-to-be dissolved convention and finished Part II of *The Age of Reason.* That autumn, before he could move on to new labors, he fell seriously ill,

Known as La belle Americaine *(the beautiful American), Eliza Monroe, wife of future President James Monroe, nursed Thomas Paine through a near-fatal illness following his release from prison.*

so much so that the Monroes believed he would not recover. Indeed, rumors spread across the Atlantic that he was dead. Yet, with Mrs. Monroe's tireless attention, Paine did recover and he immediately set himself to writing a series of critical pieces. In April 1796, he published the pamphlet *Decline and Fall of the English System of Finance*, which predicted the collapse of the Bank of England. (Fortuitously, the Bank faced a financial crisis the following year, forcing its temporary closure and delighting Paine, who imagined it might even bring down the British government and monarchy. On the latter, he was definitely mistaken.)

During this time, Paine also wrote *Agrarian Justice*, which did not appear until 1797. French developments had led Paine to see that economic inequalities were not simply a product of unfair systems of taxation and government expenditure but were also the result of unbalanced economic power and the payment of insufficient wages to working people. Even more strongly than he had in *The Rights of Man*, Paine now insisted on society's obligation to address material inequality and poverty through a system of public welfare. Specifically, he proposed a limited redistribution of income by way of a tax on landed wealth and property. He may have been influenced by Babeuf's egalitarian ideas and movement. However, as much as Paine had grown concerned about the concentration of landed property and its consequences, he did not call for changes in property arrangements or for economic democracy; he only suggested that landed property be taxed to provide for the needs of the poor.

Paine had felt compelled to write *Agrarian Justice* after reading the bishop of Llandaff's *An Apology for the Bible*, which was written as a reply to *The Age of Reason.* In his book the bishop reprinted a sermon titled "The Wisdom and Goodness of God, in having made both rich and poor." Paine opened by answering this claim: "It is wrong to say God made both rich and poor; He made only male and female; and He gave them the earth for their inheritance." Paine then argued that since God had provided the land as a collective endowment for humanity, those who had come to hold the land as private property owed those who had been dispossessed an annual ground rent to be paid in the form of a tax. Paine made it clear that he was not proposing a charity for the dispossessed but rather advocating the "right" of the dispossessed to "compensation."

Still, Paine did not suggest redistributing or recollectivizing the land. He was not a socialist; he did not contest the right of the propertied to their property. Nor did he long to restore some lost "golden age." Though he credited material progress and economic development with creating inequality and poverty ("Poverty... is a thing created by that which is called civilization. It exists not in the natural state."), he admitted that civilization had improved life in general: "the natural state is without those advantages which flow from agriculture, art, science and manufactures." There was, Paine admitted, no turning back the historical clock: "It is always possible to go from the natural to the civilized state, but it is never possible to go from the civilized to the natural state." Despite his refusal to embrace socialism, Paine's pamphlet came to be read as an early contribution to the socialist political tradition of the 19th and 20th centuries.

The last of Paine's major pieces of this period, *Letter to George Washington*, excerpts of which appeared in the U.S. press, did not well serve its author's reputation. Paine had never forgiven Washington for failing to act to secure his release from prison (though we do not know if Gouverneur Morris had ever informed Washington of Paine's predicament). Also, Washington's support of Jay's Treaty of 1794, establishing close commercial ties between the United States and Britain, appeared to Paine a betrayal of the French. Determined to vent his lingering anger, Paine composed a searing attack on Washington, questioning his principles and behavior as a general, politician, and statesman: "You slept away your time in the field, till the finances of the country were completely exhausted, and you have but little share in the glory of the final event. It is time, Sir, to speak the undisguised language of historical truth."

Washington, who remained the greatest of American heroes, never publicly responded to Paine's attack. However, the letter's publication brought forth angry responses in the United States, especially from Washington's Federalist sympathizers, whom Paine had attacked along with the first President. Washington had formally allied with no faction, but in the course of his two terms (1789–97) two political parties had emerged—the Federalists, organized by Alexander Hamilton, an author of *The Federalist Papers* and the first secretary of the treasury—and the Republicans (later to become the Democratic Party), who had gathered around Thomas Jefferson. The Federalists rallied to defend Washington, answering Paine's letter with outrage and scorn. The controversy would not easily be forgotten; many of Paine's own friends were embarrassed by his words, and the Federalists would make his eventual homecoming all the more difficult an experience.

In December 1796, with the election of the Federalist John Adams to the presidency, Monroe was recalled home, and that spring Paine moved in with the writer and publisher Nicolas de Bonneville, his wife Marguerite, and their three children. Again, it was supposed to be a temporary arrangement, but Paine would stay on for five years, that is, until his departure for the United States. The Bonnevilles welcomed Paine as a member of the family. Paine himself contributed to Nicolas's newspaper, *Le Bien informé,* and Marguerite served as a French translator for Paine.

In September 1797, when the Directory moved against the newly resurgent royalists and established its dictatorial rule, Paine actually supported its actions—no doubt surprising many. He defended his support in *Letter to the People of France and the French Armies on the Events of the 18th Fructidor—Sep. 4—and Its Consequences,* a pamphlet published by Bonneville. Believing the dictatorship to be temporary, Paine granted that such extraordinary steps were necessary as a defense against a monarchical counterrevolution: "The case reduced itself to a single alternative—shall the Republic be destroyed by the darksome maneuvers of a faction, or shall it be preserved by an exceptional act?"

In spite of everything, Paine continued to defend the original ideals and aspirations of the French Revolution, and he continued to hope that the republican movement would spread to the rest of Europe, especially to the British Isles. Increasingly, he spent his time on schemes to realize such hopes. In addition to befriending various Irish republicans, such as Wolfe Tone, and writing on the prospects for Irish revolution, he began to plan and lobby for a French invasion of Britain. The idea became something of an obsession for him, and his defense of the Directory enabled him to present his schemes to the government. Little interest was shown, except by the politically ascendant general Napoleon Bonaparte, who flatteringly told Paine that he always slept with a copy of *Rights of Man* under his pillow. "A statue of gold should be erected to you in every city of the universe," Napoleon told Paine. However, as much as Napoleon would dream of invading Britain, he would never be in a position to actually do so.

In 1798, the Directory shut down Bonneville's newspaper for having published criticisms of one of its leading figures, Emmanuel-Joseph Sieyès, a theologian who played a prominent role early in the revolution but then kept a low public profile until his election to the Directory. Paine helped Bonneville in gaining permission to reopen the paper, but it was later to be shut down again after Bonneville printed remarks understood to be critical of Napoleon. Paine himself came under increasing personal surveillance, and with the establishment of the Consulate in 1799, he again lost all faith in the Revolution.

More and more frequently, Paine spoke of returning to the United States, and he invited the Bonnevilles to accompany him, promising to bequeath them most of his U.S. properties. It greatly pleased Paine to receive the news that Jefferson had won the presidential election of 1800—defeating the incumbent Federalist, John Adams—and he thought all the more seriously about attempting the transatlantic voyage, particularly after Jefferson wrote him to offer passage on a U.S. warship. Though he did not accept the offer, Paine's return became more and more certain.

Finally, in August 1802, Paine resolved to depart France. Although Nicolas de Bonneville was forbidden by the government to leave the country, he and his wife agreed that she and the children would soon follow Paine to America and that Nicolas himself would come as soon as possible. Paine packed his belongings and, accompanied by his dearest of all friends, Clio Rickman, left for the port of Le Havre. There, on September 1, Paine and Rickman said farewell for the last time, and Paine boarded the ship *London Packet* for the journey home.

ODE TO A FRIEND

Paine's dear and longtime friend, Clio Rickman, accompained him to the port of Le Havre where Paine boarded ship for his return to America. Recognizing that this was probably their final farewell to each other, Rickman composed these lines upon Paine's sailing:

Thus smooth be thy waves, and thus gentle the breeze,
As thou bearest my PAINE far away;
O! waft him to comfort and regions of ease.
Each blessing of friendship and freedom to seize,
And bright be his setting sun's ray.

May AMERICA hail her preserver and friend,
Whose "COMMON SENSE" taught her aright,
How liberty thro her domains to extend,
The means to acquire each desirable end,
And fill'd her with reason and light.

Tho bitter, dear PAINE, is this parting to me,
I rejoice that from EUROPE once more,
From FRANCE too, unworthy thy talents and thee,
Thou art hastening to join the happy and free;
May the breezes blow gently, and smooth be the sea
That speed thee to LIBERTY's shore!

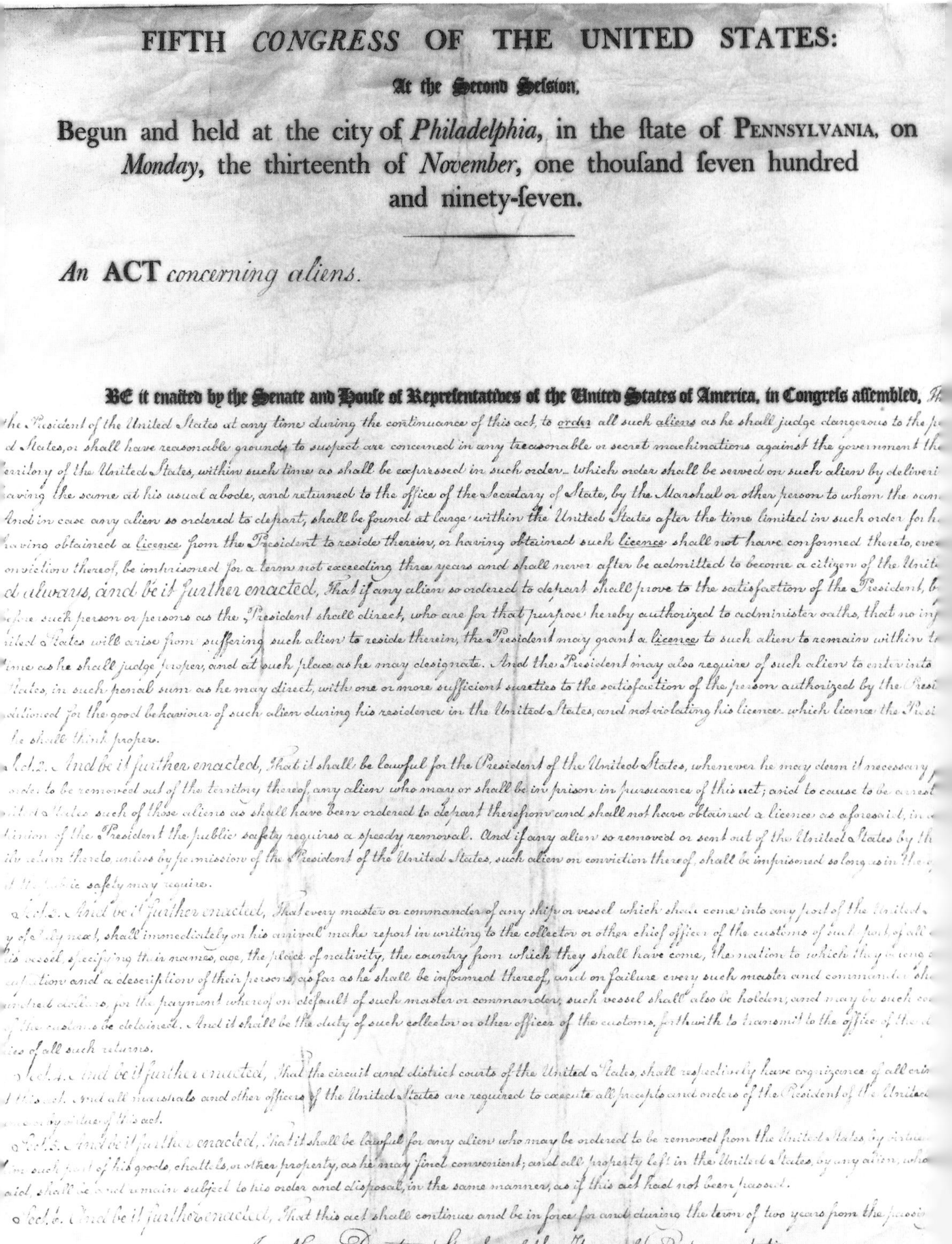

FIFTH *CONGRESS* OF THE UNITED STATES:

At the Second Session,

Begun and held at the city of *Philadelphia*, in the ſtate of PENNSYLVANIA, on *Monday*, the thirteenth of *November*, one thouſand ſeven hundred and ninety-ſeven.

An ACT *concerning aliens.*

BE it enacted by the Senate and House of Repreſentatives of the United States of America, in Congreſs aſſembled, Th

the President of the United States at any time during the continuance of this act, to order all such aliens as he shall judge dangerous to the pe

d States, or shall have reasonable grounds to suspect are concerned in any treasonable or secret machinations against the government the

erritory of the United States, within such time as shall be expressed in such order. Which order shall be served on such alien by deliveri

aving the same at his usual abode, and returned to the office of the Secretary of State, by the Marshal or other person to whom the sam

And in case any alien so ordered to depart, shall be found at large within the United States after the time limited in such order for h

having obtained a licence from the President to reside therein, or having obtained such licence shall not have conformed thereto, ever

onviction thereof, be imprisoned for a term not exceeding three years and shall never after be admitted to become a citizen of the Unit

d always, and be it further enacted, That if any alien so ordered to depart shall prove to the satisfaction of the President, b

efore such person or persons as the President shall direct, who are for that purpose hereby authorized to administer oaths, that no inj

ited States will arise from suffering such alien to reside therein, the President may grant a licence to such alien to remain within t

ime as he shall judge proper, and at such place as he may designate. And the President may also require of such alien to enter into

States, in such penal sum as he may direct, with one or more sufficient sureties to the satisfaction of the person authorized by the Presi

ditioned for the good behaviour of such alien during his residence in the United States, and not violating his licence which licence the Presi

he shall think proper.

Sect. 2. And be it further enacted, That it shall be lawful for the President of the United States, whenever he may deem it necessary

order to be removed out of the territory thereof, any alien who may or shall be in prison in pursuance of this act; and to cause to be arrest

ited States such of those aliens as shall have been ordered to depart therefrom and shall not have obtained a licence as aforesaid, in

inion of the President the public safety requires a speedy removal. And if any alien so removed or sent out of the United States by th

ily return thereto, unless by permission of the President of the United States, such alien on conviction thereof, shall be imprisoned so long as in the

the public safety may require.

Sect. 3. And be it further enacted, That every master or commander of any ship or vessel which shall come into any port of the United

y of July next, shall immediately on his arrival make report in writing to the collector or other chief officer of the customs of such port, of all

is vessel, specifying their names, age, the place of nativity, the country from which they shall have come, the nation to which they belong

cupation and a description of their persons, as far as he shall be informed thereof, and on failure every such master and commander sh

undred dollars, for the payment whereof on default of such master or commander, such vessel shall also be holden, and may be such co

f the customs be detained. And it shall be the duty of such collector or other officer of the customs, forthwith to transmit to the office of the

ies of all such returns.

Sect. 4. And be it further enacted, That the circuit and district courts of the United States, shall respectively have cognizance of all crim

this act. And all marshals and other officers of the United States are required to execute all precepts and orders of the President of the United

by virtue of this act.

Sect. 5. And be it further enacted, That it shall be lawful for any alien who may be ordered to be removed from the United States, by virtue

e such part of his goods, chattels, or other property, as he may find convenient; and all property left in the United States, by any alien, who

aid, shall be and remain subject to his order and disposal, in the same manner, as if this act had not been passed.

Sect. 6. And be it further enacted, That this act shall continue and be in force for and during the term of two years from the passi

Jonathan Dayton Speaker of the House of Representatives.

One of four acts enabling the President to limit dissent, the Alien Act of 1799 specifically authorized the government to keep foreign revolutionaries out of the country. It also enabled the Federalists to consolidate political power.

CHAPTER

10

RETURN TO AMERICA

Paine's ship sailed into Baltimore harbor on October 30, 1802. He had reason to expect a mixed reception at best. The newspapers of the day were blatantly partisan in their politics and, ever since the release of his angry letter to Washington, the Federalist press had subjected Paine to severe and foul attack. Moreover, his theses in *The Age of Reason*, especially his denunciations of Christianity, had not been forgotten. Though his Republican friends and sympathizers defended him, his enemies continued to depict him as a "lying, drunken, brutal infidel."

During Paine's 15-year absence, much had changed in U.S. politics, beginning with the adoption of the Constitution and the creation of a new government. Also, the factionalism of the postrevolutionary years had evolved into a two-party political system of Federalists and Republicans (who were later to become the Democratic Party)—the Federalists favored a strong central government and an economy based on business and industry, whereas the Republicans favored less government and championed the interests of the nation's farmers. Looking abroad, the Federalists had dreaded the radical and democratic aspects of the French Revolution, whereas the Republicans had been generally sympathetic. George Washington, who remained formally independent of both parties but increasingly leaned toward the Federalists, had served two terms as President (1789–97); John Adams, an avowed Federalist, had served one term (1797–1801); now Thomas Jefferson, the first Republican President, was serving his first term (1801–4).

Paine had always opposed factionalism. He did so first of all because he thought the cause of republicanism and democracy demanded unity against the forces of monarchy and tyranny. In addition, he feared factional politics could too easily deteriorate into a one-party dictatorship, should one of the factions fully triumph (as had happened in France). However, Paine returned to a country in which a peaceful transfer of power from a Federalist to a Republican administration had been effected. Even though he continued to fear factionalism, he remained a fighter at heart, and he too would be drawn into party battles. Though Paine had tended to support Federalist policies in the past, he returned to the United States already identified with the Republicans. This change was a consequence of his revolutionary connections in France, his friendship with Jefferson, and especially, his hostile letter to Washington, wherein he had criticized the Federalists. Though factionalism and parties never led to tyranny and dictatorship in the United States, Paine himself was to endure much nasty abuse for taking sides.

In spite of the Federalist assaults, Baltimore's citizens provided Paine a surprisingly warm welcome. A good-sized crowd greeted him dockside, and local writers recalled his contributions to America's struggle for freedom. But Federalist papers around the country fumed. Again, they made Paine out to be a "drunk," an "atheist," and a "buffoon." They also used the occasion to criticize President Jefferson for associating with Paine. Paine did not immediately respond to these ugly and derisive charges.

On November 7, he moved on to the new capital of the United States, Washington, D.C., a city still very much under construction. The press attacks continued and the reception afforded him in Washington reflected the divisions between Federalists and Republicans. Remaining a loyal friend, Jefferson enthusiastically embraced his old revolutionary comrade. In the weeks that followed, the "two Toms" passed a good bit of time together at the presidential mansion. Though it might have been politically expedient to speak critically of Paine, Jefferson never did.

In mid-November, Paine counterattacked the Federalists in an open letter titled *Thomas Paine to the Citizens of the United States*. This action firmly placed him in the Republican camp. He criticized the politics of factionalism—to which he himself was now contributing—and he held the Federalists accountable. In the ensuing weeks he composed additional letters in which he portrayed the politics of the Federalists as a menace to democracy. Referring to the Alien and Sedition Acts of 1798, which strengthened the President's authority in dealing with resident foreigners and enhanced the government's powers to suppress dissent (thereby threatening freedom of speech and the press), Paine accused former president John Adams of having imposed a "Reign of Terror."

In the early 1800s Washington, D.C., was mostly pastoral, with few buildings to house the newly relocated federal government.

Paine stayed in Washington through the winter. He was now in his mid-sixties, and his days as a revolutionary appeared to be behind him, but he did not plan merely to retire in the United States. He remained interested in international politics, and with Jefferson as President, Paine thought he might serve the U.S. government as an adviser on European affairs. He also hoped he might yet realize his dream of constructing an iron bridge. Though he was ultimately disappointed in his hopes, he never disavowed or retreated from the causes to which he had dedicated himself.

Having long believed that the United States would and should expand westward, Paine took a particular interest in the issue of the vast Louisiana territory, which Napoleon had recently secured from Spain. A crisis had erupted that very autumn when Louisiana's governor attempted to deny U.S. citizens access to the Mississippi River. Knowing that Napoleon's plans for a North American empire were unrealizable and that he desperately needed funds to finance his European military ambitions, Paine proposed that the United States buy Louisiana from France. Apparently, the U.S. government had already entered into discussions with France regarding possible purchase of the port of New Orleans. Though it is not known exactly how much influence Paine had on the negotiations, he seems to have encouraged Jefferson to revise the original U.S. position. In May 1803, the United States completed the Louisiana Purchase, buying the entire 828,000 square miles, stretching from the Mississippi to the Rocky Mountains, for $15 million.

In the winter of 1802–3, Paine also spent time reviving his scheme to build a bridge over the Schuylkill River in Pennsylvania. He arranged for his models to be shipped to Washington and presented his plans to Jefferson and members of Congress. However, neither the President nor Congress took any action (no doubt because such projects were supposed to be the purview of the states and localities). Paine made a final pitch to Congress in an essay titled "The Construction of Iron Bridges," but Congress still refused to act.

At this time, Paine received a letter regarding *The Age of Reason* from the former Patriot and founder of the Sons of Liberty, Samuel Adams. Adams, now 88 years old, registered appreciation for Paine's contribution to the American Revolution, but he expressed astonishment and dismay over what he took to be Paine's atheism. It is not clear whether Adams had actually read Paine's book, but he felt sure Paine had declared himself a nonbeliever. Paine treated the letter from Adams as an opportunity to reply to all those who had made such mistaken assertions. In an open letter he reiterated his strong and deep belief in God and restated the essential elements of his faith. Yet he also repeated both his historical criticism of organized religion—"Every sectary, except the Quakers, has been a persecutor"—and his opposition to religious dogmatism.

Paine's public reaffirmation of his deist faith and his critical stance toward Christianity invited further personal attacks, all the more so because the United States was experiencing a wave of Protestant religious fervor known as the Second Great Awakening. However, in a certain way Paine may even have contributed to the movement's advance. The Protestantism of the Great Awakening was culturally conservative in character, but—like Paine's ideas—it was also popular and democratic in spirit, challenging religious hierarchies and authorities.

In February 1803, Paine journeyed to Philadelphia, where he received a mixed reception. Some welcomed him back to his original home in the United States, but many more kept their distance, including his friend from the earliest days of the Revolution, Benjamin Rush (a devout Christian who had broken with Paine on the appearance of *The Age of Reason*). After only two days, Paine went on to Bordentown, New Jersey, where he owned a house and some property and his friend Colonel Joseph Kirkbride still lived. There he also reunited with Marguerite de Bonneville and her three children, Benjamin, Lewis, and Thomas (named after Paine), who had recently arrived from France. He granted them the use of the house and property.

In March, Paine spent a few weeks in New York. There he enjoyed himself among the city's British emigré community. He also met with James Monroe, whom he brought up to date on French developments, for Monroe was then on his way to France to work out the purchase of the Louisiana territories. At the end of the month Paine returned to Bordentown and applied himself to writing in support of Republican campaigns for the upcoming presidential and congressional elections. To his great pleasure, Jefferson and his colleagues were to win a tremendous victory up and down the country.

At the end of the summer, Paine moved north to Stonington, Connecticut, to visit with a friend, the sea captain and shipowner Nathan Haley. Paine had a splendid time. People from all over came to meet and celebrate him, and he gave a number of talks in a local tavern on politics, relations with England and France, and religion.

With the approach of winter, Paine went to check on his farm at New Rochelle. Whatever plans he had were undone by an attack of gout, an immobilizing disease involving painful inflammation of the joints. Eighteenth-century folk mistakenly believed gout resulted from heavy consumption of alcohol and bad living. So when Paine's enemies heard of his ailment, they immediately attributed it to his supposedly excessive drinking habits.

Paine did not recover until early spring, at which time he went down to New York, for he found things in New Rochelle boring. In the city he met the former Presbyterian minister Elihu Palmer. Now a deist and the organizer of the Theistic Society, Palmer established a journal, the *Prospect*, to which Paine would contribute a series of articles.

Though Paine split his time between New Rochelle and New York, he lived quite moderately. To maintain himself, clear some debts, and support the Bonneville family, he sold off part of the acreage on his New Rochelle farm and rented the remaining land to a tenant, Christopher Derrick, who also shared Paine's small cottage. Unfortunately, Paine did not get along well with Derrick, and he found it necessary to terminate the rental agreement in December 1804, evidently angering Derrick. On Christmas Eve, Derrick returned to the cottage armed with a musket and attempted to shoot Paine through one of the windows. Luckily for the surprised Paine, Derrick was very drunk at the time, and his shot missed its mark. Either out of pity for Derrick, or because he wanted to avoid a local ruckus, Paine did not press charges.

In 1805, Paine drew up plans to produce a six-volume collection of his writings. The idea may have originated as a means of raising money, but Paine had far more in mind. Worried that succeeding generations of Americans would forget the radicalism that had inspired their revolution and, as a result, fail to remain vigilant against the rise of tyrannical authority, he wanted to cultivate a republican and democratic spirit among them. He believed that making his writings more readily available would help keep alive the prophetic memory of the struggles of 1776. However, Paine's advancing age diminished his energies and prevented him from carrying out the necessary editing. Instead, he worked on smaller literary projects, most notably, letters to Jefferson on the Haitian Revolution and the possibility of settling poor blacks on the Louisiana Purchase lands, and a short pamphlet, *Constitutions, Governments, and Charters,* published in the summer of 1805.

Through the remainder of the year, Paine made every effort to write, but he realized he could not work as he had before, and he worried that his funds were running out. He felt responsible not only for himself but also for Marguerite de Bonneville and her children. He grew depressed and perceived himself abandoned by the world. Increasingly, he did take to serious drinking.

In the spring of 1806, Paine's friend William Carver, a New York blacksmith, came to visit. Finding Paine in terrible physical condition and his cottage in complete disarray, Carver insisted that Paine come to live with him and his wife in the city. By summer Paine's health and spirits had improved. However, on July 25, he suffered a stroke. The Carvers thought he would die, but he made a remarkable recovery and—though bedridden until October—was quite soon back to reading newspapers, arguing with visitors, and drinking. The Carvers found Paine less and less bearable. Unfairly—they had invited him to stay as a guest—they presented him with a bill for his stay and their services. Paine refused to pay.

In mid-November, Paine moved in with a 26-year-old artist, John Wesley Jarvis, who just the year before had pleased Paine by painting a portrait of him. The arrangement greatly suited Paine, and he remained Jarvis's housemate into the spring. However, Paine occasionally experienced acute loneliness, for the young bachelor Jarvis spent most evenings out at taverns, often in the company of women, and usually returned home in the early hours of the morning.

In April 1807, Paine moved to the outskirts of the city to reside in rented rooms at the home of a politically sympathetic baker, Zakarias Hitt, and his family. During the next year Paine kept up his writing, addressing matters such as the defense of New York's harbor. He also wrote to Congress in hopes of securing reimbursement for his services to the cause of independence. But his efforts failed, making him feel all the more aggrieved and abandoned.

In February 1808, Paine moved out of the Hitt home to rooms above a less-than-reputable tavern. Close friends who visited him were horrified at the state in which he lived; Paine's rooms and possessions were a mess. That summer, a few of them took the liberty of arranging residence for him with Mr. and Mrs. Cornelius Ryder on Bleecker Street in Greenwich Village, then a district just to the north of the city. To make ends meet, Paine sold off his Bordentown property.

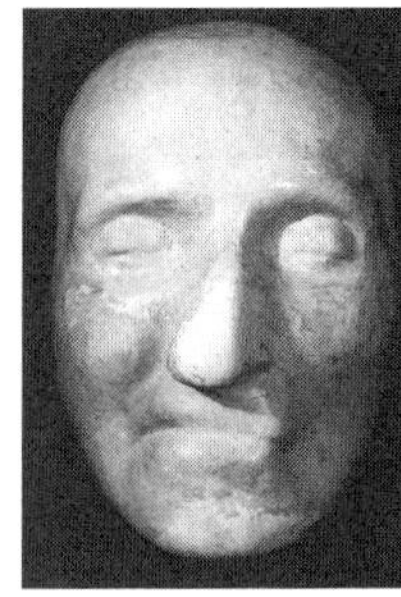

Friends of Paine observed that his death mask was "remarkable for its fidelity" to his features. Marguerite de Bonneville said, "Death had not disfigured him.... Though very thin, his bones were not protuberant. He was not wrinkled and had lost very little hair."

In January 1809, Paine drew up his will, keeping his promise to Nicolas and Marguerite de Bonneville. He determined that on his death his New Rochelle farm was to be divided: the northern section of land to be sold, the proceeds going to Nicolas and Clio Rickman, and the southern section, along with the shares of stock he held in the Phoenix Insurance Company of New York, to be given to Marguerite. Paine also stipulated that he should be buried in a Quaker cemetery with his headstone bearing his name, age, and the words "Common Sense."

Paine's health continued to decline. He developed fevers and stomach swelling. Marguerite de Bonneville visited him every other day. Those close to him did not expect him to live much longer. Further devastating him, in March the New Rochelle Quaker community rejected his request to be interred in their burial grounds, for they feared that Paine's admirers would make his gravesite a place of pilgrimage and would seek to erect a monument there, which would be contrary to their beliefs. Marguerite de Bonneville promised to arrange burial on his New Rochelle property, in reply to which Paine observed that later owners of the land would probably "dig up my bones before they are half rotten."

In April, in order to tend to him herself, Marguerite rented rooms on nearby Grove Street, to which she had Paine transferred. There he continued to receive visitors, some welcome and some not so. The latter included individuals who, knowing the old radical was near death, hoped to get him to recant his deism in favor of Christianity. But Paine denied them any satisfaction. On June 8, 1809, he died, holding firmly to his own beliefs.

"Tom Paine," a B-17F Flying Fortress, was stationed near Thetford in 1943. The inscription under the name reads, "Tyranny, like hell, is not easily conquered." Units of the U.S. Eighth Air Force placed a plaque on a wall in front of Thetford's town hall bearing the inscription: "This simple son of England lives on through the ideals and principles of the democratic world for which we fight today."*

CHAPTER

11

Remembering Paine

Tom Paine's funeral took place in New York on June 9, 1809. Very few attended. Marguerite de Bonneville, as she had promised, arranged for Paine's burial on his New Rochelle farm. No public dignitaries or statesmen were present, and no eulogies were offered when Paine's coffin was lowered into the ground. Sadly, Mme. de Bonneville later recalled:

> This interment was a scene to affect and to wound any sensible heart. Contemplating who it was, what man it was, that we were committing to an obscure grave on an open and disregarded bit of land, I could not help feeling most acutely. Before the earth was thrown down upon the coffin, I, placing myself at the east end of the grave, said to my son Benjamin, "stand you there, at the other end, as a witness for grateful America." Looking round me, and beholding the small group of spectators, I exclaimed, as the earth was tumbled into the grave, "Oh! Mr Paine! My son stands here as testimony of the gratitude of America, and I, for France!" This was the funeral ceremony of this great politician and philosopher!

Paine's burial may have passed without commotion, but even in death he would not be ignored. He had played too important a role in the making of the modern world to be easily forgotten. Rejecting the expectations of the age, he helped to turn a colonial rebellion into a revolution and to gird its protagonists against the onslaughts of empire. At the same time, he instilled republican values and egalitarian sensibilities in his fellow citizens and endowed them with a sense of their nation's exceptional promise. Opposing the power of the privileged and propertied, he encouraged workingmen on both sides of the Atlantic to demand equal democratic rights and to wonder about the political and social causes of economic inequality. And, repudiating the dogmas and bigotries of the day, he argued in favor of religious pluralism and the separation of church and state.

Even John Adams, Paine's revolutionary friend but later antagonist, grudgingly acknowledged that the remarkable times in which they lived likely would—and should—be known as the times of Tom Paine. In 1805, Adams wrote to a friend, using words of insult that Paine himself might have read as praise:

> I am willing you should call this the Age of Frivolity as you do, and would not object if you had named it the Age of Folly, Vice, Frenzy, Brutality, Daemons, Buonaparte, Tom Paine, or the Age of the Burning Brand from the Bottomless Pit, or anything but the Age of Reason. I know not whether any man in the world has had more influence on its inhabitants or affairs for the last thirty years than Tom Paine. There can be no severer satyr on the age. For such a mongrel between pig and puppy, begotten by a wild boar on a bitch wolf, never before in any age of the world was suffered by the poltroonery of mankind, to run through such a career of mischief. Call it then the Age of Paine.

Paine truly was, and remains, the greatest radical of this revolutionary age—an age that rulers, aristocracies and elites have long tried to declare over, but have repeatedly failed to halt or escape. The struggles for freedom, equality, and democracy that engaged his imagination and pen have continued, and they have been extended and deepened. In ways Paine himself might well have appreciated, his life and ideas have been called upon to serve these ideals.

During the 19th century, and for much of the 20th, democrats, labor organizers, socialists, and religious free-thinkers kept alive Paine's memory and the arguments he advanced in *Common Sense*, *Rights of Man*, *The Age of Reason*, and *Agrarian Justice*. In his native Britain, Paine remained a celebrated hero of radical artisans and the new industrial working classes. When the Chartists formed the first British working-class political party in the 1830s, their manifesto stated that their activities would entail "disseminating the principles propagated by the great philosopher and redeemer of mankind, the immortal Thomas Paine." And, ever since, British labor activists and socialists have regularly called forth Paine and his principles in support of trade-union and democratic causes. Moreover, his words challenging British imperialism encouraged not only 18th-century Americans to fight for an end to colonialism; they also inspired 20th-century rebels, such as the independence leader and first prime minister of India, Jawaharlal Nehru.

In his adopted country, the United States, Paine's career and writings have influenced generations of radicals—arguably, he is the progenitor of the American radical tradition. Working-class political parties of the 1820s and 1830s held commemorative dinners every year on Paine's birthday. Figures such as feminist Fanny Wright, poet Walt Whitman, and labor leader and socialist Eugene Debs drew inspiration from Paine's vision of America. Also, two 19th-century presidents, Andrew Jackson and Abraham Lincoln, well remembered for their democratic fortitude and spirit, openly admitted to their admiration for the author of *Common Sense.*

Paine has not been universally revered. Although in the 1980s American conservatives came to appreciate Paine because of his criticisms of governmental power and his defense of individual enterprise, for much of American history conservatives resisted granting Paine a place in the pantheon of the nation's Founding Fathers. Many despised his memory and sought to suppress it, especially businessmen who worried that Paine's ideas might further instigate working people and minorities to demand equal rights and powers, and religious fundamentalists who refused to understand or tolerate Paine's religious beliefs. In 1888, future President Theodore Roosevelt referred to Paine as a "filthy little atheist."

However, radicals and progressives did not defer to such views. In the 1930s, American labor organizing and radical politics surged in the face of economic depression, widespread poverty and unemployment, and the rise of European fascism and dictatorship. Writers and performers enthusiastically advanced Paine's memory in support of union organizing drives and workers' struggles. For example, in 1939, renowned singer and actor Paul Robeson performed Earl Robinson and John Latouche's "Ballad for Americans"—a song fully recognizing Paine as a founder of the nation—on national tour and on radio. In 1943, the writer Howard Fast published his historical novel *Citizen Tom Paine*, and in 1945 the historian Philip Foner published the most complete edition (to date) of Paine's writings. In his Washington's Birthday "fireside chat" on radio in 1942, President Franklin Delano Roosevelt conjured up images of the troops at Valley Forge and recited Paine's opening words in *The American Crisis* to fortify the nation for the hardships posed by U.S. entry into World War II.

The 1960s witnessed a similar revival of interest in Tom Paine and the American Revolution, as a consequence of the dramatic campaigns for the civil rights of African Americans—a movement looked upon by many as the Second American Revolution—and the demonstrations protesting American involvement in the Vietnam War. Sociologist and social critic C. Wright Mills, whose writings powerfully influenced the students who mobilized in the American New Left, had often referred to Paine in his work. And the ensuing bicentennials of the publication of *Common Sense* and of the American Revolution itself led to further assessments of Paine's role in history, including Eric Foner's *Tom Paine and Revolutionary America* (1976).

In the wake of the Cold War and the collapse of old certainties and political ideologies, scholars, journalists, and activists once again have turned to Paine in search of fresh and critical ideas about securing or advancing freedom and democratic life. Along with increasing references in historical and political studies to Paine's contributions to American thought and development, major Paine biographies and new editions of his writings have appeared. Plus, with the advent of cyberspace, several World Wide Web sites have been dedicated to Paine, and media critics have invoked his name in defense of on-line freedom of speech. We often find Paine and his arguments advanced to the fore of intellectual and public discussion, and with people of all political stripes now making claims on his legacy, the contest for his memory has been lively.

Devoted admirers have established societies and built monuments to honor Paine's memory. Britain's Thomas Paine Society, formed in 1963, has held regular gatherings and commemorative events. British and American folk musicians have included the Paine-inspired Irish melody "The Rights of Man" on their latest recording collections, and still others have composed original songs about him. And, in Lewes, England, where Paine began his life in public affairs, the local beer company prepares a special "Tom Paine" brew every July to honor him and the American Revolution.

In the United States, the Thomas Paine National Historical Association, founded in 1884, has maintained Paine's cottage in New Rochelle as a museum. Statues of Paine have been erected in Thetford, Paris, New Rochelle, Bordentown, and Morristown, New Jersey. In 1968, Paine's image adorned a U.S. postage stamp, and, in 1992,

text continues on page 149

A Legacy of Inspiration

Although Paine would long be scorned by the powerful and propertied, generations of radicals kept his memory alive and were inspired by his ideals. Throughout his life, American poet Walt Whitman often spoke affectionately of Paine and his ideas on politics and religion. In 1877, Whitman delivered the address "In Memory of Thomas Paine" at Lincoln Hall in Philadelphia on the 140th anniversary of Paine's birth. In his remarks, Whitman highlighted Paine's contribution to the making of the United States, and he urged his fellow citizens not to forget those, like Paine, who have struggled to preserve and advance American freedoms.

In Memory of Thomas Paine.... That he labor'd well and wisely for the States in the trying period of their parturition, and in the seeds of their character, there seems to me no question. I dare not say how much of what our Union is owning and enjoying today—it's independence—it's ardent belief in, and substantial practice of, radical human rights—and the severance of its government from all ecclesiastical and superstitious dominion—I dare not say how much of all this is owing to Thomas Paine, but I am inclined to think a good portion of it decidedly is....

He served the embryo Union with most precious service—a service that every man, woman and child in our thirty-eight States is to some extent receiving the benefit of to-day—and I for one here cheerfully, reverently throw my pebble on the cairn of his memory. As we all know, the season demands—or rather, will it ever be out of season?—that America learn to better dwell on her choicest possession, the legacy of her good and faithful men—that she well preserve their fame, if unquestion'd—or, if need be, that she fail not to dissipate what clouds have intruded on that fame, and burnish it newer, truer and brighter, continually.

Congress approved plans to create a Paine monument on the Mall in Washington, D.C.

There is, however, no actual Paine gravesite to visit. As Paine himself had foreseen when he was denied a Quaker burial, his bones were to be disinterred from his New Rochelle property. But the event was more complex than Paine could ever have imagined. In 1819, the English radical journalist William Cobbett—who, strangely enough, had written critically of Paine in the 1790s—announced his determination to restore Paine to Britain:

> Paine lies in a little hole under the grass and weeds of an obscure farm in America. There, however, *he shall not lie, unnoticed, much longer.* He belongs to England. His fame is the property of England; and, if no other people will show, that thay value that fame, the people of England will.

On an autumn evening of the same year, Cobbett, his son, and another man dug up Paine's coffin without permission and, before they could be stopped, hurriedly transported it to New York City, where they loaded it on board a ship bound for Liverpool.

But history would not have it that Citizen of the World Paine could so easily be claimed by England, or by any other single country. Stories differ as to what precisely happened next. Some say that on Cobbett's return he displayed Paine's bones in Liverpool and then put them in a warehouse, where they were lost. Others insist that Cobbett's son sought to have the box of bones auctioned off in 1835, on his own father's death, but the auctioneer refused to follow his instructions. Paine's remains are said to have subsequently disappeared. Either way, they are nowhere to be found.

Other tales are also told. Perhaps the most appropriate recounts that on the trip back to England, Paine's coffin slipped overboard in a storm. It seems only fitting and just that Tom Paine should be resting somewhere between Britain, France, and America.

Chronology

1737
Thomas Paine born January 29 in Thetford, England

1743
Enrolled in Thetford Grammar School

1750
Apprenticed to his father to learn craft of corset making

1757
Enlists to serve aboard the privateer *King of Prussia*

1759
Becomes master corsetier; marries Mary Lambert, who dies the following year

1762
Secures commission as excise officer

1765
Dismissed from Excise Service; pursues a series of jobs in London and attends scientific lectures

1768
Re-appointed to Excise Service and posted to Lewes

1771
Marries Elizabeth Ollive

1772
Leads Excise Officers' campaign for higher salaries

1774
Excise Officers' campaign fails; dismissed again from Excise Service; marriage ends in separation; departs for America

1775
Appointed editor of *Pennsylvania Magazine*; composes "The Liberty Tree"

1776
Publishes *Common Sense*; joins the Continental Army and writes *The American Crisis*

1777
Appointed secretary to Committee on Foreign Affairs

1778
Becomes embroiled in Silas Deane affair

1779
Resigns as secretary to Committee on Foreign Affairs; appointed Clerk of the Pennsylvania Assembly

1781
Travels to France to secure further aid for American cause

1783
Treaty of Paris ends Revolutionary War; Paine increasingly engages in scientific matters, especially the design of an iron bridge

1787
Travels to France in hope of securing financing for his iron bridge; returns to England to visit widowed mother and to seek English support of bridge project

1789
French Revolution begins July 14

1791
Traveling back and forth between London and Paris, writes Part One of *Rights of Man* in defense of the French Revolution

1792
Publishes Part Two of *Rights of Man*; British Government seeks to prosecute Paine for sedition; elected to French National Assembly; avoids arrest in England; convicted in absentia of "seditious libel" in London

1793
Writes first part of *The Age of Reason*; at Christmas, arrested and imprisoned

1794
Becomes seriously ill; release secured by new American minister to France, James Monroe; re-elected to National Convention

1795
Publishes second part of *The Age of Reason*; writes *Agrarian Justice* (published 1797), outlining a system of public welfare

1797
Writes in favor of the cause of Irish independence from Britain

1800
Thomas Jefferson elected President of the United States

1802
Returns to America

1803
Spends time in New York City and on his farm in New Rochelle

1806
Moves to New York City; health declines

1809
Dies on June 8; buried on his farm in New Rochelle

Further Reading

Biographies

Dyck, Ian, ed. *Citizen of the World: Essays on Thomas Paine.* London: Helm, 1987.

Foner, Eric. *Tom Paine and Revolutionary America.* New York: Oxford University Press, 1976.

Fruchtman, Jack, Jr. *Thomas Paine: Apostle of Freedom.* New York: Four Walls Eight Windows, 1994.

Hawke, David Freeman. *Paine.* New York: Norton, 1974.

Keane, John. *Tom Paine: A Political Life.* London: Bloomsbury, 1995.

Collections of Paine's Writings

Foner, Eric, ed. *Thomas Paine: Collected Writings.* New York: Library of America, 1995.

Foner, Philip, ed. *The Complete Writings of Thomas Paine.* 2 vols. New York: Citadel, 1945.

Foot, Michael, and Isaac Kramnick, eds. *The Thomas Paine Reader.* New York: Penguin, 1987.

The Age of Revolution

American Social History Project. *Who Built America?* Vol. 1. New York: Pantheon, 1989.

Bernstein, Richard B., with Kym S. Rice. *Are We to Be a Nation?:The Making of the Constitution.* Cambridge: Harvard University Press, 1987.

Bobrick, Benson. *Angel in the Whirlwind: The Triumph of the American Revolution.* New York: Simon & Schuster, 1997.

Butler, Marilyn, ed. *Burke, Paine, Godwin and the Revolution Controversy.* Cambridge: Cambridge University Press, 1984.

Countryman, Edward. *The American Revolution.* New York: Hill & Wang, 1985.

Gilmour, Ian. *Riot, Risings and Revolution:Governance and Violence in Eighteenth-Century England.* London: Hutchinson, 1992.

Hobsbawm, E. J. *The Age of Revolution,* 1789–1848. London: Weidenfeld & Nicolson, 1962.

Jaffe, Steven H. *Who Were the Founding Fathers?* New York: Holt, 1996.

Mack, Stan. *Stan Mack's Real Life American Revolution.* New York: Avon Books, 1994. (Cartoons)

Maier, Pauline. *American Scripture: Making the Declaration of Independence.* New York: Knopf, 1997.

McCrory, Martin, and Robert Moulder. *French Revolution for Beginners.* London: Writers & Readers, 1983.

O'Brien, Conor Cruise. *The Great Melody: A Biography of Edmund Burke*. Chicago: University of Chicago Press, 1992.
Palmer, R. R. *The Age of Democratic Revolution: A Political History of Europe and America, 1760–1800*. 2 vols. Princeton: Princeton University Press, 1959.
Porter, Roy. *English Society in the Eighteenth Century*. New York: Penguin, 1990.
Rediker, Marcus. *Between the Devil and the Deep Blue Sea: Merchant Seamen, Pirates and the Anglo-American Maritime World, 1700–1750*. New York: Cambridge University Press, 1987.
Rudé, George. *Europe in the Eighteenth Century: Aristocracy and the Bourgeois Challenge*. London: Weidenfeld & Nicolson, 1972.
———. *The French Revolution*. New York: Weidenfeld & Nicolson, 1988.
———. *Hanoverian London, 1714–1808*. London: Secker & Warburg, 1971.
———. *Ideology and Popular Protest*. Chapel Hill: University of North Carolina Press, 1995.
Thompson, E. P. *Customs in Common*. New York: New Press, 1991.
———. *The Making of the English Working Class*. New York: Vintage, 1963.
Wood, Gordon. *The Radicalism of the American Revolution*. New York: Knopf, 1992.
Young, Alfred F., ed. *The American Revolution*. De Kalb: Northern Illinois University Press, 1976.
———, ed. *Beyond the American Revolution*. De Kalb: Northern Illinois University Press, 1993.

REMEMBERING PAINE

Fast, Howard. *Citizen Tom Paine*. 1943. Reprint, New York: Evergreen, 1983. (Fiction)
Zinn, Howard. "Pamphleteering in America," in Greg Ruggiero and Stuart Sahulka, eds. *Open Fire*. New York: New Press, 1993.

MUSICAL RECORDINGS

Bragg, Billy. *Don't Try This at Home*. Elektra, 1991. Includes "North Sea Bubble," remembering Tom Paine and his revolutionary ideals.
The Chieftains. *Bonaparte's Retreat*. Shanachie Records, 1989. Includes the Irish hornpipe melody "The Rights of Man."
Phillips, Barry. *The World Turned Upside Down*. Gourd Music, 1992. Includes "The Rights of Man."
Robeson, Paul. *Ballad for Americans and Great Songs of Faith, Love, and Patriotism*. Vanguard Records, 1989. Includes "Ballad for Americans," by Earl Robinson and John Latouche.
Tilson, Steve, and Maggie Boyle. *All Under the Sun*. Rounder Records, 1996. Includes a musical appreciation, "Here's to Tom Paine."

INDEX

Page numbers in *italic* refer to pages with illustrations.

Acknowledgments

In the preparation of this work, I depended most heavily upon three outstanding biographies: Eric Foner's *Tom Paine and Revolutionary America* (Oxford University Press, 1976); Jack Fruchtman, Jr.'s *Thomas Paine: Apostle of Freedom* (Four Walls Eight Windows, 1994); and particularly John Keane's *Tom Paine: A Political Life* (Bloomsbury, 1995). In addition to the other works listed in the suggested readings, I also drew upon Alyce Barry, "Thomas Paine, Privateersman," *Pennsylvania Magazine of History and Biography* 101 (October 1977), 451–61, and Alfred F. Young, "Common Sense and the Rights of Man in America: The Celebration and Damnation of Thomas Paine," in Kostas Gavroglu, ed. *Science, Mind and Art* (Kluwer Academic, 1995).

I must also acknowledge the assistance and encouragement of Isaac Kramnick, Al Young, Eric Foner, Marcus Rediker, and Richard Bernstein; the editorial commitment and support of Nancy Toff, Editorial Director of Trade and Young Adult Reference at Oxford University Press in New York, and her colleagues, Casper Grathwohl and Karen Fein; and the critical engagement of my in-house editors, my wife Lorna, Rhiannon, and especially Fiona.

Picture Credits

American Antiquarian Society: 26; American Philosophical Society: 50; British Museum: 88; Chicago Historical Society: 53; Guildhall Library, Corporation of London: 16; Library of Congress: 8, 19, 20, 23, 28–29, 30, 31, 35, 42–43, 48, 56, 62, 68, 70, 77, 78, 86, 89, 93, 97, 102, 104–105, 111, 112, 124, 126, 135; Library of Virginia: 13; National Archives: 132, 142 (United States Air Force Photo Collection); National Portrait Gallery, London: cover; Collection of The New-York Historical Society: 141; New York Public Library, General Reference Division: 94, 116, 122; New York Public Library, Rare Book Collection: 66; By courtesy of the Trustees of Sir John Soane's Museum: 84–85; Thomas Paine National Historical Society: 82.

Text Credits

General of the Headstrong War, p. 37: Reprinted in John Keane, *Tom Paine, A Political Life*. Boston: Little, Brown, 1995, p. 69.

"The Liberty Tree," 1775, pp. 52–53: Reprinted in Michael Foot and Isaac Kramnick, eds. *The Thomas Paine Reader*. New York: Penguin, 1987, pp. 63–64.

Ode to a Friend, p. 131: Reprinted in John Keane, *Tom Paine, A Political Life*. London: Bloomsbury, 1995, p. 452.

A Legacy of Inspiration, p. 148: Reprinted in Justin Kaplan, ed. *Walt Whitman, Poetry and Prose*. New York: Library of America, 1982, pp. 821–23.

Harvey J. Kaye is the Ben and Joyce Rosenberg Professor of Social Change and Development and Director of the Center for History and Social Change at the University of Wisconsin-Green Bay. He is the author of *The Powers of the Past, The British Marxist Historians, "Why Do Ruling Classes Fear History?" and Other Questions*, and *The Education of Desire*, which was awarded the Isaac Deutscher Memorial Prize. He is the editor of several major works, including *History, Classes and Nation-States, Poets, Politics, and the People, The Face of the Crowd*, and *The American Radical.* He is a regular contributor to the *Times Higher Education Supplement* and a variety of other American and British periodicals.